John Dooley
Confederate Soldier
HIS WAR JOURNAL

Edited by JOSEPH T. DURKIN, S.J.
Professor of American History,
Georgetown University

Foreword by
DOUGLAS SOUTHALL FREEMAN
Author of *R. E. Lee, Lee's Lieutenants,* etc.

THE UNIVERSITY OF ALABAMA PRESS
Tuscaloosa

The University of Alabama Press
Tuscaloosa, Alabama 35487-0380

Published by The University of Alabama Press, 2005

∞
The paper on which this book is printed meets the minimum requirements of American National Standard for Information Science—Permanence of Paper for Printed Library Materials, ANSI Z39.48-1984.

Library of Congress Cataloging-in-Publication Data

Dooley, John, 1842–1873.
John Dooley, Confederate soldier : his war journal / edited by Joseph T. Durkin ; foreword by Douglas Southall Freeman.
p. cm.
Originally published: Washington : Georgetown University Press, 1945.
Includes bibliographical references and index.
ISBN 0-8173-5265-1 (pbk. : alk. paper)
1. Dooley, John, 1842-1873. 2. Confederate States of America. Army. Virginia Infantry Regiment, 1st. 3. Virginia—History—Civil War, 1861–1865—Personal narratives. 4. United States—History—Civil War, 1861–1865—Personal narratives, Confederate. 5. Soldiers—Virginia—Biography. I. Durkin, Joseph T. (Joseph Thomas), 1903– II. Title.
E581.51st .D66 2005
973.7'455'092—dc22

2005003789

CONTENTS

FOREWORD

THE lesser narratives of the War between the States sometimes explain the larger. Nearly always the problem of the historical student is not the *what* but the *why*, not the event, but the reason for it. In many such cases, official documents do not give the solution. The reporting officer may have delayed so long the preparation of his account that his explanation of a particular decision or the cause of a critical twist of action became confused in his mind. More often, obscurities and omissions covered failures. On occasion, too, if the reported outcome of a battle conforms too closely to an officer's elaborate account of what he intended to do, suspicion is aroused that afterthought is presented as forethought. To avoid the temptation of pretending that the contingent was part of the original design presented a test, always, of a soldier's intellectual honesty.

Where, for any of these reasons, the report of a Union or Confederate fails to answer the student's question, the narrative of a junior officer or the diary of a private may. A rain that is not mentioned in the report of the commanding General may have turned a road across a lowland into a quagmire. Unconfessed failure of commissary officers to get food to the front, a bad road block, lack of water, stifling dust on a long march, the sore feet of men who had to march over hard roads after days on sandy byways —these circumstances, which may have decided battles, occasionally are set forth, sometimes casually, in the personal narratives of inconspicuous soldiers.

To such narratives, also, a student must turn if he is to understand the morale of an army. From those narratives one often gets color and incident and a thousand touches that lighten the unrelieved seriousness of official reports. Half-a-dozen narratives, written by privates or sergeants of Lee's Army, are as important as the collected reports of any brigade commander or of almost any divisional leader. One thinks particularly of John O. Casler, of William W. Chamberlaine, of David Johnston, of Edward A. Moore and of John H. Worsham.

Most acceptably, to these familiar books, and to others of the same type, there now is added this narrative of a soldier of the First Virginia Infantry, Kemper's Brigade, Pickett's Division, First Corps Army of Northern Virginia. The journal of John E. Dooley begins immediately after the battle of Cedar Mountain, Aug. 9, 1862, and closes so far as it describes combat, with the charge of July 3, 1863, at Gettysburg. There is an interesting and wholly-authentic addendum on prison life, but the most valuable part of the story John Dooley tells from the viewpoint of a private and then of a company officer is that which covers the eleven red months of offensive operations between the Rappahannock and the Susquehanna. It was the period of the greatest achievements of Lee's Army. In all of them, except Chancellorsville, the men of Kemper's brigade had an honorable role, sometimes a conspicuous part. As narratives by soldiers of Pickett's Division are few, that of John Dooley complements Johnston's *Story of a Confederate Boy in the Civil War* and deserves the editorial care Father Durkin has spent on it.

The dual form of the manuscript, a diary and an expanded narrative, is one used by several Confederate writers. In Father Durkin's presentation of the text, about four-fifths of the entries are from the original diary. The passages elaborated by Captain Dooley are distinguished easily. In some published diaries, this is not always possible. George M. Neese's *Three Years in the Confederate Horse Artillery*—to cite a single example—is a readable narrative concerning a branch of the service poorly documented; but the contemporary entries and the subsequent rewriting and adornment so impair the historical testimony that it puzzles the reader. Captain Dooley's additions to his diary were made, fortunately, while the events themselves still were fresh in a youthful mind. He probably erred in attempting to rewrite his journal, because he occasionally indulged in heroics; but he did not mislead himself nor will he mislead his reader with incidents that imagination draped when time and failing memory had left fact dim and drab.

The vice Captain Dooley avoided without difficulty has misled many an autobiographer and many a historical writer who relied too confidently on personal narratives written late in life and long after the events. Individual memory varies much. No historical canon, therefore, can be applied uniformly. In general, experience has shown that incidents of a dramatic character, first put in print two decades or more after their occurrence, should not be accepted unless confirmed by some earlier authority. This is particularly true in those instances where a public man who made numerous speeches subsequently wrote them down. So apt was the orator to "adorn the tale" that the usual historical critique may not suffice to save the reader from acceptance of error. In the case of John Dooley, his flourishes, which are not numerous, are literary and not factual. They do not impair a narrative which Father Durkin has edited with so much judgment and scholarship that one gladly steps back, so to say, and presents him to the audience.

DOUGLAS SOUTHALL FREEMAN

INTRODUCTION

THIS is the simple record of an unimportant Confederate soldier who fought in the War Between the States. It is not a treatise on tactics or strategy by a military expert; it is not the work of a trained historian; it is, rather, the unadorned but vivid story of how the war, the men, and the times looked to one in the ranks, who frequently had thoughts and feelings very different from those of the generals. It has also a message for the present: it tells of citizen soldiers who, in their gay humor, their courage, their disinclination to be called heroes, remind us of our own boys in twentieth century wars.

The author is John E. Dooley, youngest son of John Dooley and Sarah Dooley, both of Limerick, Ireland, and later of Richmond, Virginia. They were cousins, having come to America in the same ship in that year of mingled promise and foreboding — the beginning of the second term of President Andrew Jackson, 1832. When they landed in Baltimore, the 'Young America' movement, with its brilliant hopes and golden dreams, was in full ascendancy; the West was still in the making; the first railroad had just been built; but there was also, in the debate over the Ordinance of Nullification of South Carolina, the low but ominous rumblings of what could indeed have been called an "alarm bell in the night."

John and Sarah had probably met for the first time on the voyage across the ocean. They were married at Alexandria, Virginia, in September 1836, and, that same year, took up their abode in Richmond. They were oppressed by no premonitions of armed strife within the country to which they had come as a refuge. Richmond of the 'forties and 'fifties was a gracious and friendly place in which to live. Some of its families traced their lineage back to the first settlers; they were aristocrats of the blood, but they were free from the not uncommon infirmity of aristocracy, snobbishness. Many a newcomer could have echoed the words of Edmund Walls, who, at the end of his happy and prosperous life in the city, left a rich monument "in token of gratitude to the citizens of Richmond, for their kindness to him who came among them a poor boy." [1] So, as John Dooley's business of furrier and hatter grew rapidly, as God blessed them with numerous children, and as they became a respected and beloved family in the metropolis of the South, they must indeed have felt that the hopes with which they had come to America were being abundantly fulfilled.

By 1862 they had two sons and five daughters. One daughter had died in infancy. The eldest boy, George, they had lost just before the outbreak of the War. The children were, in order of age: Mary, James, John (the author of this journal), Alice, Florence, Sarah, and Josephine.

The family was by this time one of the wealthiest and most popular in Richmond. Their home was the recognized center of a social group whose importance has never been sufficiently appreciated — the Irish-Americans of the prewar South. The Dooley door was ever open to Irishmen who came to America to enjoy the blessings of free citizenship in a free republic. The Irish political exile John Mitchel was an intimate friend of John Dooley. Indeed, the latter typified neatly the fusion of two distinct but mutually

[1] Quoted from Foreword by Douglas Freeman in *Richmond Virginia in Old Prints, 1737-1887* (ed. Alexander W. Weddell and John L. McElroy), Richmond, 1932, xxiv.

complementary national loyalties when in April 1861, at the head of his Company, the Montgomery Guards, he marched out of Richmond in a uniform of vivid bottle-green with gorgeous gold stars and bars.[2]

John Dooley was obviously a sound practical man of business; for he came to America a poor immigrant, yet, within twenty years, his family occupied a place in the upper society of Richmond. He was also, according to a contemporary account, the "kindest and most generous of men." [3] While commanding his company in the war, it is said that he "often on a bitter, cold night could be seen bringing the men on guard a drink, saying with a smile, 'I saw you wink at me'." [4] His love for his wife and children was of a distinctive tenderness.[5] He was gregarious; in his new home he loved to entertain elaborately. It is clear, too, that he had a passionate love for the land where he had found the opportunity to live out his life in freedom; this land was the South.

As for Sarah Dooley, a few sentences in letters of her son John, written three years after the close of the war, throw a significant light on her character. He wrote, "You have always been, dear Mother, a great sufferer and your Merits

[2] A proof of the devotion of these Irishmen to the country of their new allegiance is found in the epitaph on the tomb of John Mitchel at Charleston, S.C.: "I could not fight for Ireland, so I chose to fight for the South." Two of his three sons were killed in the War Between the States. His third son became the father of John Purroy Mitchel, future mayor of New York.

[3] Charles T. Loehr, *War History of the Old First Virginia Regiment, Army of Northern Virginia,* Richmond, 1884, 15.

[4] *Ibid.*

[5] He wrote home from Chicago, whence he had gone on a business trip: "Dearest Sarah: . . . This is the longest time I have been yet from home and I never have been so anxious to get back. . . . Kiss all the children for me. . . . Your more than ever devoted Husband, J. D." (John Dooley to Sarah Dooley, Chicago, Aug. 12, 1857.)

on this account must be great before God. Ever since I remember anything, you have never been free from pain and illness. . . ."[6] Again, in his letter of condolence on his father's death, he urges her to bear up under the grief, "for their sakes who have always looked up to you for counsel and consolation in their doubts and trials."[7] From all the evidence, and despite her delicate health, she was the typical valiant Irish mother, glorying in those jewels, her children; judging, too, from the traits of her sons and daughters, we may safely surmise that she possessed those lovely adornments of the women of Ireland — sweetness, gaiety, and personal charm.

The sons and daughters of John and Sarah Dooley united the moral wholesomeness, ruggedness, and marked individuality of the Gaelic character with the mellow, silk-brocade-and-candlelight culture of the Old South. They were not, of course, without their faults, but they were warm, human people, with distinct personalities of their own. Mary, one of Richmond's popular belles, married Robert McCandlash Jones, her brother's 'buddie' during the war. Some memories of their courtship, in the stately measure of Richmond society of the 'sixties are found in Robert's handwriting on some of Mary Dooley's music sheets. To the title of the song, "Still in My Dreams Thou'rt Near" he has added, "Yes, often!"; the title, "Queen of My Soul" has the comment, "Yes indeed you are!"; and to "Change Not Thou," the wooer has playfully appended, "Never! Don't you!"

Florence and Josephine also married happily. Alice remained single, devoting herself unselfishly to her mother in

[6] John E. Dooley to his mother, from Georgetown College, Feb. 9, 1868.

[7] John E. Dooley to his mother, from Georgetown College, Feb. 24, 1868.

the latter's declining years. Sarah ('Sadie') took the veil as a Visitation nun, becoming later Superioress of the Visitation convent in Richmond. James became, after the war, a wealthy businessman and a most generous benefactor of the city of Richmond. His last testament was his greatest eulogy, for it witnessed to his love of the poor.

As to John, it will be best to let him reveal himself in this journal, which is almost as much a delineation of his own character as it is a transcript of his experiences in the war. His sister, Mrs. Josephine Houston, still living in 1944, remembered him, of course, quite clearly. She told the present writer that John was (to use her own words) "always the life of the house," and that "he was always thinking of something sweet to do for somebody." He seems also to have been, in his very young days, something of a little aristocrat. Mrs. Houston recalled that John on his way home one day from dancing school saw the mother of one of his little girl friends hanging out clothes on the line. John's patrician sensibilities were, apparently, shocked. On reaching home he exclaimed incredulously to his mother, "Ma, 'Liza Plumes' mother *works*!"

There was nothing remarkable about his boyhood. He did most of the things that were being done by the normal boys of Richmond in those bygone days, except that his somewhat delicate constitution kept him out of the more vigorous outdoor games. He seemed to have a happy faculty for getting the maximum enjoyment out of life. There was about him, however, a touch of seriousness somewhat beyond his years, as is evidenced by his liking for books with such formidable titles as 'Sheil's History of the Irish Bar.' He displayed, too, that traditional and forgivable trait of the younger brother — a fondness for teasing his sister about her beaux. Interspersed with Robert Jones' more gallant observations on Mary's song sheets are some waggish interpolations in John's handwriting. He has added, "Then it's *not* so true!" to the song title 'My Heart's on the Rhine,' and scribbled "*Was* he mournful?" after the title 'O Sing Again That Mournful Lay.'

In the fall of 1856 John, at the age of 14, entered Georgetown College. Of this period of his life we have few records. From a letter to his father, written in 1858, we know that even thus early he was interested in military matters; for he tells of his being elected as Second Lieutenant in one of the cadet companies which the Southern boys had organized on the campus.[8] He gives also the rather enigmatic information that "the other day, when I wouldn't go to the first meeting of the 'Cricket Club,' the boys just *in spite* elected me vice president." [9] He never graduated from college, since he interrupted his studies early in 1862 to enlist in the Confederate Army. At the conclusion of the war he returned to Georgetown, this time as a Jesuit novice. Further details of this latter period of his life will be given in the Epilogue to his journal.

No sketch of the Dooley family would be complete without mention of a factor which loomed large in the lives of the father and his two sons — the Old First Virginia Infantry Regiment, termed by the outstanding scholar of Southern military history the "most famous regiment in the history of the United States Army." [10] At various times, though not

[8] John E. Dooley to his father, from Georgetown College, Oct. 17, 1858. It is not clear whether he participated in the celebrated incident of February 1861, when the Southern students of Georgetown insisted on burning Mr. Abraham Lincoln in effigy on the campus (cf. W. Barnum, "Notes on Georgetown College and Trinity Church at the beginning of the War, 1861, and the following year," *Georgetown University Archives,* 128/4).

[9] John Dooley to his father, from Georgetown, Oct. 17, 1858.

[10] Conversation of Dr. Freeman with the editor.

simultaneously, the three Dooleys served in this unit. One of its companies was, for the first nine months of the War Between the States, led by John's father, who was in fact, during the latter part of the winter of 1862, acting commander of the whole regiment. John's brother James fought as a private in the First Virginia until seriously wounded in the battle near Williamsburg, May 5, 1862. The fortunes of the regiment, from the summer of 1862 to the end of the war, were most intimately intertwined with the history of the author of this journal.

It was indeed a famous regiment. Its ancestry dated back to the earliest known muster of the Virginia colonial militia at Westover, July 12, 1661, although its existence as a corporate military unit began on February 16, 1754.[11] In its first engagement, on the Great Meadows, May 28, 1754, it was commanded by George Washington. During the Revolution it was led for awhile by Patrick Henry. Becoming a part of the Continental Line in August 1776, it fought in the battles of Trenton, Princeton, and Monmouth, and was in the Southern campaign, including Yorktown. It saw action in the War of 1812, and was with General Taylor at Monterey in the Mexican War.

At the outbreak of the War Between the States the various companies of the 'Old First' were in the field among the very first. Its 'C' Company, in 1861, was commanded by John Dooley's father. At the first battle of Bull Run the

[11] For the history of the regiment the editor is indebted to the following work by Captains John C. Weckert and Henry G. Dickerson: *The 'Old First' Virginia Infantry: an Outline History: the Military Apprenticeship of George Washington* (supplement to *The Rattlesnake*, Richmond, 1933). On the occasion of the unveiling of the monument to the 1st Virginia Regiment in 1930, these two authors made special researches into the history of the organization. They uncovered so much material that it was incorporated in a series of supplements to the above-named periodical.

regiment held its ground against two Yankee brigades, and at the close of the day was master of the field. For its part in this action it won the high praise of Generals Robert E. Lee and Longstreet.[12] From the fall of 1861 until the spring of the following year it was active in the campaigns in Northern Virginia. It lost heavily in the battle of Seven Pines, May 31, 1862, but assisted in driving the Federals back in that fight. It took part in the Seven Days Battle around Richmond, where it suffered further losses. The author of this journal joined the regiment in August 1862. He could truly feel that in doing so he was carrying on a double tradition — that of the oldest military unit in what had been, until April 1861, the United States Army, and that of two generations of Dooleys who had fought under the standard of the "Old First."[13]

[12] In the effects of Mrs. Josephine Houston was the original of John Dooley's father's will, written the day before the first battle of Bull Run. It runs in part as follows:

> July 18, 1861. I, John Dooley, of the city of Richmond, but now at Bull Run River, (hourly expecting a battle with the Northern enemy), knowing at all times, but particularly under present circumstances, the uncertainty of life, do now make this my Will, which is all in my own handwriting. Having the fullest confidence in the sound discretion of my wife, Sarah, I do hereby give, devise, bequeath and dispose of unto her all my property, real and personal, and of every kind and description, with power should she find it necessary to sell all or any portion of my real estate, and to convey the same to purchaser or purchasers, trusting to her in the management of everything and to the making of such disposition of my estate at such time, in such manner and in such proportions among our children as she may deem best for their interest. . . . It is especially my wish and desire that my mercantile business shall be carried on as usual if it is at all practicable, but of this my wife must be the judge. . . .

[13] For more details of the history of the regiment, *vide* Appendix III.

A word regarding the editorial method followed in this book:

During his active service in the field as a member of the 1st Virginia Regiment, from August 1862 to July 3, 1863, John E. Dooley kept a day-by-day account of his experiences; this diary comprises *Dooley's War Notes, series I,* in the Georgetown University Archives. Some portions of this diary he rewrote and elaborated during his detention at the Federal prison on Johnson's Island, from mid-summer of 1863 to March 1865; still other portions he recast and expanded during his residence at Georgetown from 1865 to 1873. Both these later revisions constitute *Dooley's War Notes, series II,* in the Georgetown University Archives.

The present Journal is a composite of these two series, with series I comprising approximately four-fifths of the volume. Wherever it was deemed helpful, the editor has inserted into the day-by-day account passages from series II. The first few instances of such fusions are indicated by footnotes; subsequent instances are marked by asterisks at the beginning and end of the passage from series II.

The editor has tried to make a minimum of alterations in Dooley's text. Some sections of the original have been omitted, on the ground that such excision of material merely repititious or obviously unimportant would contribute to a truer over-all picture of the events and conditions which the author is seeking to describe. These omitted parts are indicated by the conventional broken line, and in some cases a brief résumé of the omitted passage or passages has been added in a footnote.

In a few instances Dooley's spelling has been rectified: in most cases it has been left unchanged. More liberty has been taken with his punctuation, which, for the reader's convenience, has been considerably revised, though not in every instance. There was an evident need for explanatory footnotes, which have been provided; also chapter titles and running heads in the text have been added.*

The first edition of the book was published on a grant from the Sitterding Foundation, established by two devoted Georgetown University alumni, Mr. Fred B. Sitterding, Jr., and Mr. William H. Sitterding. Important research aids were provided by the beloved priest and citizen of the New South, Monsignor Thomas A. O'Connell, of Richmond. Miss Adele Clark, of the same city, was helpful because of her wide knowledge of the history of the Dooley family.

But the person who really inspired the book was Douglas Southall Freeman, the greatest scholar and one of the most admirable gentlemen the present writer has ever known. Freeman had devoted his professional life to a study of Robert E. Lee and George Washington; and his long vicarious contact with them had refined and enriched his own character. He was a man of honor, principle, and very great gentleness. He once left on a young scholar whose name may be guessed an impression of nobleness that the years have not effaced. The editorial advice of this master of Southern military history was the most precious boon received by John Dooley's manuscript.

It seems significant that this second edition of John Dooley's diary appears during the observance of the Civil War Centennial. His loyalty to the South was equalled only by his devotion after 1865 to the United States of America. Symbolically, he became in his last years a teacher in a

* Dooley's intermingling of past and present tenses has frequently been left uncorrected.

college which chose as its colors a blend of Blue and Gray.

JOSEPH T. DURKIN, S.J.
Georgetown University,
September 8, 1962

Chapter One

". . . WHILE ALL WE HAVE MOST DEAR . . ."

ONE day in April 1861 a small group of students filed solemnly into the office of Father John Early, president of Georgetown College. Obviously nervous, yet with a quiet determination, they laid before the president a written petition. All these boys were from the South; and the document they were presenting was an urgent request that they be relieved of their studies and allowed to return home. The petition was quite explicit, and, in its simple way, eloquent. This was the heart of it:

> Our presence here any longer would be attended but with little good to us, for . . . there is not one amongst us who is now able to devote that time, interest, and energy and requisite spirit to the pursuit of our classes, . . . while all we have most dear on earth, our Country (the South), our parents and our brethren call loudly upon our presence at our respective homes.[1]

There is no record of Father Early's response; but a few months later every one of these young men was serving in the Confederate Army. Some of them, before two years had passed, had paid the supreme sacrifice.

In that same Spring of 1861 John E. Dooley was a Freshman at Georgetown. Although, with the rest of his classmates, he was thrilled at the firm action taken by the petitioners, he realized that he was too young to enlist. A year later, however, the case was different. He was now 19; his father and his elder brother James were already fighting

[1] J. T. Durkin, *Glimpses of Old Georgetown*, Washington, 1939, p. 43. The original of this document is in the Georgetown University archives.

in the war; so John concluded that it was no time to be conning Latin Grammars or writing Greek themes. Whether or not he presented his request formally to Father Early we do not know. But in early June of 1862 he is wearing a Confederate uniform and performing some rather undramatic duties as a kind of military policeman in his native city. He was not satisfied, however, with this service behind the lines. His diary begins at this point.

I HAD been in the Confederate Service one month and a half, only, but, tired of remaining in the City catching deserters and conscripts, I resolved at once to enter the field where I considered it the imperative duty of every young man to be. Altho' repeatedly warned that I was doing a rash thing, that I would never be able to undergo the fatigue and hardships of a soldier's career, and that I would come back in a very few weeks 'kilt entirely,' nevertheless I was resolved to make the experiment, cost what it might, and on the morning of the 12th of August I left Richmond to join the 1st Reg't. of Virginia Infantry, Kemper's Brigade, Longstreet's Corps, then stationed near Gordonsville.[2]

The day was broiling hot, and my companion Capt. James Mitchell[3] and I were obliged to clamber to the top

[2] The general strategic situation in northern Virginia at this time was as follows: The Union General John Pope had begun his drive towards Richmond, and had reached the Rapidan about twenty miles north of Gordonsville. He planned to effect a junction of his forces with those of McClellan, who was reported to be moving westward from the vicinity of Fredericksburg. General R. E. Lee, seeking to crush Pope's army before the two Union forces could come together, sent ten Brigades under Longstreet to reinforce Stonewall Jackson at Gordonsville. John Dooley joined his regiment just in time to take part in this latter movement.

[3] These first few pages are from Dooley's War Notes, series II.

of the train, the inside of which being completely crammed by Gen. Pryor's Brigade who were being transported to Gordonsville. My wardrobe consisted of a change of clothing wrapped in a blanket, and my weapon, for I had but one, was a tolerably respectable Springfield musket.

We arrived in the evening of August 12 within a few miles of the Camp of the 1st Brigade [Kemper's], and proceeded at once to the 1st Regt.[4] The bloody battle of Cedar Mountain (Augt. 9) had just been fought and won by the Confederate forces under Genl. Stonewall Jackson,[5] and the boastful Pope was taking position for a new stand against the army of Genl. Lee, which was being rapidly concentrated in the vicinity of Orange C.H.

The first sight that attracted my inexperienced eye upon approaching the bivouacks of our army was the burial of some of the heroes who had fallen two days before[6] at Cedar Mountain. It was anything but encouraging to a heart which naturally shrank from deeds of blood and scenes of death to behold these mangled heroes dropped carelessly in to the graves prepared, and the cold earth flung by colder hands upon their mutilated forms. I turned half sick from the ghastly spectacle and thought that I, too, before another day passed by, might be numbered with the dead and rudely thrust beneath dear Mother earth.

The Brigade had just returned from a most harassing

[4] Longstreet's Brigades (including Kemper's) were not yet at Gordonsville, but would be sent there by Lee on the 13th. Cf. Douglas Southall Freeman, *Lee's Lieutenants: a Study in Command*, 3 vv., N. Y., 1942–1944, II, 53. The 1st Virginia Regiment had arrived at Gordonsville on the 10th.

[5] That the battle of Cedar Mountain was not really a Confederate victory has been shown by Freeman, *op. cit.*, II, 43–47.

[6] Rather, three days before.

wild goose chase, having been thro' the hot sun nearly all day twelve or fifteen miles in search of the enemy, and then returned to camp worn out by their march and almost parched by the intense heat of the day. Some of the members of the Regt. guided us to our place of bivouack and we were cordially welcomed by the remnants of the 1st. Regt.

The Decimated First

I call them remnants because at this period the regiment was reduced to the paltry number of 66 men, less than the number of a good company. At first the Regt. had, I think, 1100 men and eleven companies. 5 companies had been removed; out of the remaining six many of the members being mechanics by trade had been detailed by the government for special duties;[7] many had enlisted but for one year and many had been killed and wounded in the various battles from Bull Run down to the present days.

These sixty-six soldiers were already veterans in a noble cause, and loved oftentimes to dwell on the scenes of their past warlike adventures. Bull Run, Yorktown, Williamsburg, Seven Pines, Mechanicsville, Cold Harbor, Frayser's Farm and Malvern Hill were inscribed on their tattered

[7] The Confederate Government's handling of its manpower problem was apparently not without flaw. A Sergeant of Company D, 1st Va. Inf. Reg't., wrote as follows: ". . . Most of the men of the regiment having a mercantile or mechanical education, contractors and those in charge of the Confederate offices were daily making applications to the War Department for some member of the regiment to fill positions of trust, or where mechanical skill was needed. As a rule the request was granted, and thus the Confederate War Department detailed the men faster than the officers could get new recruits. It became at last discouraging to the officers, and all the efforts of the commanders in the field failed to correct the evil. The need of such men at the capital was given as the excuse." (Charles T. Loehr, *War History of the Old First Virginia Regiment, Army of Northern Virginia*, Richmond, 1884, 15, note.)

banner; and their fields red with their own and the blood of their comrades in arms might furnish inexhaustible matter for chat as they gathered around the blazing log of the campfire or loitered on the green grass or in the pine grove bivouack during the slowly creeping hours of the summer night. . .[8]

We were asked many questions about the latest from Richmond, etc., and soon after partaking of some bread and make-believe coffee we prepared to retire to rest.

I felt strange enough, I assure you, lying down this my first night in camp. The strange faces and forms, the near and distant sounds of an army of men talking, shouting, singing, and all upon different subjects; the croaking frogs, cries of the Whip-poor-Will, the glare of the camp fires and the neighing of horses and the deep shadows of a dark night overhanging all; all these were not calculated to allay my uneasiness of mind or lighten my heart of its cares.

But others were sleeping and why should I not do likewise? So, kneeling for a few moments I said some brief prayers and lay me down in peace and quietness; for my Guardian Angel was watching by my side, and, though I little suspected it then, bore me through many a dreadful peril even to this hour.

Two years afterwards Lieut. K.[9] of my Company told me that he watched me the next night to see if I would again go down on my knees, and when he did not see me do so he conceived rather a poor opinion of me and also of my religion. I of course felt exceedingly mortified, and my only excuse was that I did not wish to appear too

[8] As explained in the Introduction, some omissions of Dooley's text have been made by the editor. In each instance such omissions will be indicated by a broken line.

[9] Lieutenant William H. (Peter) Keiningham. Dooley later refers to him as 'Pete' *Kunningham*.

singular in my habits, so I deferred saying my prayers until I lay down. He was not satisfied, however, nor was I, with myself, although I had that portion of the Scriptures on my side when our Lord counsels his followers to pray in secret.[10]

The next morning after laving in a neighboring brook and having taken some *Army* breakfast, I felt more at home and was 'duly' installed in my new position of Soldier in Company D, Cap't. Geo. Norton, 1st Va. Infantry.

We were here but two days when that grand movement began which resulted in the defeat of Gen. Pope at Manassas and the expulsion of the invading army from Northern Virginia.[11]

[10] At this time, judging from the bits of evidence at our disposal, John Dooley was not physically prepossessing. He was somewhat below the normal stature for a man, and weighed about 130 pounds. His health had never been robust, and he had not engaged in much outdoor exercise. He was naturally shy and of very delicate sensibilities; one is tempted to term him over-sensitive. He had always, however, been well-liked by his associates, both male and female, and his Richmond friends who called him 'Gentleman Jack' had used the sobriquet in the spirit of real compliment. He had a boyish charm, and he made friends easily. A stranger, meeting him today, would probably catalogue him as a nice boy from Richmond, trying very hard to be a man. For this and other information concerning Dooley the editor is indebted to Mrs. Josephine Houston, John's sister and only surviving member of his immediate family. The Journal itself gives some hints of the author's personal appearance; cf., for instance, p. 176.

[11] Waiving, for the moment, the questions as to who was really defeated at Manassas, and which army was expelled from northern Virginia, it will be well to review briefly the over-all strategic situation in Virginia in that mid-August, 1862. The concentration of Lee and Longstreet on Gordonsville by August 15 had imperiled Pope's position north of the Rapidan. In the sector northeast of Gordonsville the Rappahannock and the Rapidan formed a 'V', narrowing in the direction of Fredericksburg. Into this 'V' the Federal commander was being crowded by the arrival of the Confederate forces at Gordonsville. If Lee could effect a cavalry encirclement of Pope's right, and destroy the railroad bridge across the Rappahannock, the Union leader would be cut off from his

We began our march upon the 16th of August.[12] Our army moved slowly along the dusty high roads, and the searching rays of a midsummer sun played fiercely on our heads and blazed straight in our dust bespeckled faces. I knew that being a raw recruit in the ranks my fellow comrades naturally thought I would not be able to withstand the long fatiguing marches, the dusty roads, hot broiling sun, sleepless nights, the mountain dews, the slender rations and drenching rains. I knew also that my delicate appearance would naturally beget suspicions of weakness on my part; and I suspected on theirs that there was a certain feeling of jealousy which all or nearly all brave soldiers feel towards those whom they suspect of shirking duty in the field or even in the least degree seeking their comfort at home when they might be useful elsewhere.

Dooley Keeps On Marching

Seeing or thinking that I saw such suspicions and feelings among my fellow-soldiers (although outwardly I was treated with the utmost kindness by all with whom I associated), I would rather have dropped dead on the road side than to have broken down in the midst of our hardships and fatigues or have missed the first glorious battle in which we so soon became engaged.

---

base. This movement Lee decided to attempt; but, in order to screen it and to throw Pope off balance, the Confederate commander-in-chief determined to ford the Rapidan on the night of August 17 and to attack Pope on the 18th. (This explanation follows closely Freeman, *op. cit.*, II, 56–57.) Kemper's Brigade, with John Dooley plodding along in the ranks, was one of the units assigned to this crossing of the Rapidan.

[12] On the night of the 15th-16th the 1st Va. had camped near Mechanicsville, Louisa County. On the 16th they marched north on the Orange and Fredericksburg Turnpike, passed through Orange Court House, and, on the 20th, crossed the Rapidan at Raccoon Ford. Cf. Loehr, *op. cit.* p. 26.

As we passed near Orange Court House, Gen. Kemper's mother is sitting on the front porch to greet us as we go. She is bent with years and silvered are her tresses bound up in neat simplicity; but she waves her kerchief to her son's brave troops and bids them Godspeed against a relentless and unprincipled foe. Twelve miles were all we marched today[13] and it was enough for me, being my first march; and I was glad, when the shades of evening gathered round, to throw my wearied body beside the road and prepare for rest.

Next morning after snatching a hasty repast we are on the dusty high road again and the sun grows hotter and hotter.

*Day after day and night after night did we tramp along the rough and dusty roads; 'neath the most broiling sun with which the month of August ever afflicted a soldier; thro' rivers and their rocky valleys, over mountains and thro' rocky glen—on, on, scarcely stopping to gather the green corn from the fields to serve us for rations. Oh, how often when the midday sun poured down his fiercest beams, how often when my weary legs, feeling like lumps of bruised flesh, mechanically as it were, moved one after the other (at the dead of night), how often was I tempted to lay down my musket and acknowledge myself conquered by the numberless hardships and terrible fatigue of the Campaign. But I felt it my duty to endure every thing and above all my pride sustained me; and from the bottom of my heart I was wont on occasions of such temptations to ask of God to give me renewed strength to enable me to complete that arduous Campaign. During these marches the men are

[13] This is the first instance of the author's shift to his day-by-day entries. In his journal he will henceforth intersperse these entries with his recollections written soon after the events. *Vide supra*, Introduction, p. xxi.

oftentimes unrecognizable on account of the thick coverings of dust which settle upon the hair, eye-brows and beard, filling likewise the mouth, nose, eyes, and ears; and the poor victims are much like hard toiling millers, although *much more so.**

Marching Through Virginia

Sometimes the road leads through the woods and then how delightfully cool we feel, how lustily we cheer and sing our chorus with redoubled enthusiasm; for one of the chief helps in our company towards keeping up gaiety and a cheerful heart is to march in time to some popular air which we all sing in chorus and repeat over and over again. I really think, nay I am sure, that half the fatigue of a march may be avoided or unfelt if the men have music to cheer their drooping spirits and enliven their lagging steps.

Miles upon miles of desolate track may be seen every day through fertile fields which should be teeming with rich harvests of luxuriant grain, but now also they are trodden under foot by ruthless foes whose retreating steps are scarcely more destructive than the march of their avenging pursuers. Here the fences thrown down and the rails half burnt; the smoking homestead and the houseless, breadless orphan appeal to heaven for retribution upon a wanton cowardly foe whose brutal orders have been but too faithfully executed by a depraved and savage soldiery.

*This contemptible apology for a general, Pope, kept us following upon his heels for ten or twelve days,[14] and it

[14] Lee's plan to catch Pope in the 'V' was wrecked by Fitz Lee's failure to join Stuart until night of the 18th at Verdiersville. Fitz Lee then notified Gen. R. E. Lee that his forces were not in condition to act against Pope on the 19th. The commanding general therefore deferred the advance of the Army until the 20th. By that time, Pope had taken alarm, crossed the Rappahannock, and escaped from the 'V'. Cf. Freeman, *op. cit.*, II, 60–61.

was not until Jackson's little army had gone round him, intervening between his army and Washington that he could be induced to stand his ground.[15] Our marches were constant and nearly always prolonged into the night.

Keeping the Army on the Move

One day I was sent some distance back to see if our wagons were very far behind, and if possible to bring them up with the Regt. I found the road in our rear blocked completely by wagons of every description, commissaries', quartermasters', ordnance, etc., etc. The train extended to the rear at least ten or fifteen miles and our wagons were some three or four miles from our position and I was informed that all these wagons had their proper place in line and could not, even though there was room on the road, leave the position assigned them. Our men were taking up their line of march and I was told to remain behind and bring up the wagons.

Hence I had a fine view of nearly the whole of Longstreet's Corps. I stood upon a slight eminence and watched each brigade as it left in column last night's bivouack and marched towards a mill race which flowed nearly at the bottom of our slope. It was a glorious sight to see this little army, in so many divisions, approaching and crossing this stream at several points. The sun burst out from the heavy mist which had enveloped it, and glancing along the guns and accoutrements of the soldiers, filled meadow, hill and

[15] "Jackson, on the morning of August 25 was despatched with 25,000 men on a forced march, his aim being to cross the Rappahannock above the position of the Union army, to move through Thoroughfare Gap, strike the Orange and Alexandria Railroad in Pope's rear, and sever his communications with Washington." (James F. Rhodes, *History of the United States from the Compromise of 1850*, 8 vv., N. Y., 1904, IV, 122). The next day, August 26, Longstreet, John Dooley accompanying, followed on Jackson's trail.

stream and heart with blithesome gaiety. How they shout and sing and laugh and joke while brigade after brigade pass by and ford the stream. Few care how wet they get; necessity urges and what must be done they'll do quickly.

All the morning they were passing this stream, and to my inexperienced eye there appeared at least a hundred thousand men. But I learned afterwards that we had not at most more than thirty thousand in this corps.

Some Trouble With the Wagons

The wagons are passing at another portion of the Stream, and I stand waiting for ours to make their appearance, but in vain. Nearly every second wagon comes to a halt in the middle of the stream, which is deep, and the wagons are heavy and the horses, unlike the wellfed beasts of the Yankees, are weak and they must drink; and so there is much ado about getting out of the stream and clambering up the ground on the other side of which is any thing but a level plain.

There I waited until late in the evening for our Regimental train to come up, *but it didn't come.* (I wish some of the wiseacres at home who sit in their cozy offices and write censorial articles about the inefficiency of Generals in failing to follow up their victories and in annihilating this and t'other army could have stood where I did on that memorable day and watched the slow process of this immense train of wagons which was almost steadily passing here all day and at night fall scarce one half had crossed the little stream. They [the armchair strategists] might then understand what it is to move a large army over rough, muddy, and rocky roads, having but one road for troops, baggage, ordnance, ammunition, Quartermaster's stores and Commissaries.

The Problem of Transport

In other countries where every part of the state is connected by railroads or smooth turnpikes, and the greatest perfection in the management of the necessary supplies, ordnance, etc. has been attained, we have no doubt often noted and admired the rapidity of the movements made by immense armies and their astonishing celerity in following up their successes. But to any one who watched the progress of our army and the immense wagon trains, etc., absolutely necessary for its maintenance, it must have been evident that (en masse) celerity of movement was not and could not be (with either defeat or victory) our forte.

I grew weary watching wagon after wagon as it passed this little stream, and still no sign of our own; I decided that our teams would come along just as quickly were I there or not; so I abandoned my post, following the road the army had taken, and trusting to come up with our men during the night*. . . .[16]

A Traitor and a Spy

Before I leave this vicinity let me tell you that two men were hung at Stephensburg by a drum head court martial, Gen. Longstreet commanding. The 1st of these men was a deserter, a West Virginian, and had been a captain in our army last year. Yesterday he was found in Stephensburg, recognized by his old companions, tried, condemned, and executed. The other was a Yankee spy of remarkable daring. Gen. Lee, it appears, had dispatched a courier (a private of Hampton's Legion, many of whom wore a dingy-brown uniform) to General Longstreet to take various posi-

[16] The author rejoins his Corps at Brandy Station, on the Orange and Alexandria Railroad. Longstreet's Brigades are now pursuing Pope in a northeasterly direction. Jackson is ahead of Longstreet by about a day's march.

tions at the different fords in the Rappahannock which the enemy might occupy to prevent our crossing. The Yankee spy intercepted the courier in a lonely spot, killed him, took his dispatch and dressed himself in the dead man's brown suit of clothes. Hastening on to Gen. Longstreet he, instead of presenting the orders, announced verbally that the Gen. should march in an almost totally different direction from that commanded. Longstreet was perplexed, the courier is detained. An officer on the General's Staff (formerly of the Hampton's Legion) does not recognize the courier, the body of the murdered courier is found, and the spy is tried, condemned, and executed. . . .

Longstreet Continues the Pursuit

We are now in Rappahannock County[17] and are pressing on after the enemy, and have taken this circuitous route[18] purposely I think in order not to drive him straight before us but to press him gradually into the old position of Bull Run and Manassas Junction.

Our Lieut. Col. (Skinner) is an old Baltimorean and lives in this county. The Col. has always been noted in the army for his good natured blustering manner, slashing his sword in a most terrible way when a near combat with the enemy is spoken of. He is very well educated, having spent many years in Paris, and speaks French fluently.[19]

[17] On August 23 the 'battle of Rappahannock' was fought by the 1st Va. It was principally an artillery engagement, the infantry, apparently, not being involved. Dooley makes no mention of this incident. See also p. 8, note.

[18] Longstreet, following Jackson, kept bearing to the west slightly, in the general direction of Warrenton and Thoroughfare Gap, instead of moving in a straight line against Pope.

[19] Frederick Gustavus Skinner was one of the most romantic and gallant characters of the war. As a boy he had been sent to Paris by his father, a warm friend of the Marquis de Lafayette, to be educated in

Last year when the Prince Napoleon[20] visited our army at Manassas, Col. Skinner was one of those who acted as his escort and entertained him. As our Regiment was being reviewed by the Prince, the latter remarked to Col. Skinner when our men had passed by, that the *seats* of the soldiers' *breeches* seemed very much the worse for wear. 'That is true', replied Col. S., 'But I assure you, *their enemies know nothing about that*'.

Closing in on Pope

Tonight (Aug. 27th) we cross the northern branch of the Rappahannock, the ford being quite deep and the crossing taking place between 9 and 10 P.M. We have marched pretty rapidly today and bivouack late in the night, arising before day-break, 28th Augt., to continue our march. The enemy cannot be far distant now and there are evident signs of great caution and anxiety through the whole corps.

This is a hard day's march and we arrive at dusk near the little town of Salem.[21] Here we thought we would have

---

the great Frenchman's household. He remained there ten years and attended the famous military school of St. Cyr. Later he graduated also from West Point. A chronicler of Southern manners has described him thus: "[He was] a figure who attracted swift attention whenever duty brought him to Richmond. . . . Immensely tall, great-boned and of tremendous strength, his grave, intellectual face swept by a drooping gray mustache, this soldier was a marked man in any throng. Cadet of an old Virginia family, he was still a thorough Frenchman in many respects. . . . He was a strange combination of reckless courage, bluntness, and urbanity, . . . a gourmet by instinct. . . . He was called by Charles King 'the grandest old lion of all Rebeldom' " (T. C. De Leon, *Belles, Beaux and Brains of the 60's*, N. Y., 1909, 247–249). John Dooley will later describe Colonel Skinner's astounding bravery at the Second Battle of Manassas.

[20] This was Joseph Charles Paul Bonaparte (Plon-Plon).

[21] Longstreet's Corps had followed on Jackson's trail, with the aim of uniting with him and thus closing the circle around Pope. By August

a rest, but no; forming in good order we passed through the little town where all is bustle and excitement. Staff officers and couriers are dashing up and down the street (I believe it has only one), ladies are waving their kerchiefs from the lighted windows, and more than one voice is heard at the piano singing fortissimo 'Dixie', 'Bonnie blue flags', etc. This was all very cheering, but it would have been more so had we been halted and quartered for the night in those brilliantly lighted parlours and had joined our voices with those who swelled those patriotic lays.

Alarm in the Night

We crossed the Manassas Gap railroad and camped for the night in an open field. Fires might be made, but no noise, for the enemy were close at hand. I was nearly exhausted with fatigue and while fires were lighted for miles around and the men prepared a little coffee, I prepared to sleep, seeking a clean spot near 'Tantie' Jones[22] and Capt. Mitchell.

Silence gradually crept through our wearied encampment (and many slept soundly all around.) How long I slept I do not know; but suddenly I hear a cry of terror borne along the field, and the whole camp, bright with its blazing fires, seemed in wild commotion. Snatching my musket I jumped to my feet but was hurled instantly to the ground while some larger object tore by with lightning speed (so it appeared to me.) Almost senseless and bruised

28 Longstreet was at Salem, and Jackson was at Bull Run, awaiting the arrival of Longstreet. At mid-night of August 28, Pope's van reached Manassas, only to find that Jackson had flown. Pope was being gradually forced into the position at Manassas, where he would soon be obliged to make a stand.

[22] Sergeant-Major R. M. Jones of Richmond, close friend and messmate of Dooley. He later married John's sister, Mary.

from head to foot I lay where I had been thrown until Tantie and Capt. Mitchell raised me up and rubbed my bones and joints, examining to see if ought was fractured, finding that I was only bruised and stunned.

I was much relieved in mind although very sore in body. What struck me? I thought at first that it was the cavalry of the enemy who were not far off. But it happened that two of the General's staff horses, becoming terrified at the blazing flames roaring and crackling too near them, broke their fastenings and plunged wildly over the sleeping masses of soldiers. The cries and shouts of those in danger and of those who wished to warn, increased the terror of the animals which sped like the wind across the entire bivouack, wounding and creating the greatest consternation among the half awakened soldiers. I escaped more luckily or providentially than many others. The horse striking me (with his *fore*—not four—hoofs) in the breast stunned and stiffened me, but the only damages I could discover were some long scratches from the breast down to the knees. One poor fellow in Co. G had his collar bone broken and a large portion of his ear torn off. Another had his arm broken, others received serious bruises and wounds, and in many other regiments many other soldiers received serious wounds.

Morning dawns upon the field of last night's disaster. What, thought I, if a brigade of the enemy's cavalry had charged thru our bivouack instead of two unsaddled horses? I feel unable to walk when I first try to rise, but being helped to a neighboring stream and performing my morning ablution, I feel a little refreshed and after limping about a little while I grow less stiff and am resolved not to be left behind, if I can possibly keep up.

CHAPTER TWO

SECOND MANASSAS AND AFTERWARDS

AFTER hastily taking some coffee we are on the tramp again, following the rail road track and approaching 'Thoroughfare Gap' which is about a mile from our last night's bivouack. This 'Gap' on the Manassas road lies between two high and rocky eminences which might easily have been held by a few brave men against a large force. Had the enemy known what they were about they might have here checked Longstreet's corps and compelled him to make a detour through another gap above, by which delay Jackson's gallant little army, now in imminent danger, might have been destroyed.[1] As it happened, the enemy left but a small force to defend the gap, who fled at the first attack and this formidable position was forced yesterday evening by one of our advanced divisions.

DOOLEY'S FIRST BATTLE

Passing through this morning (Augt. 29), several Blue coats who were killed last evening are lying scattered here and there unburied. Things begin to look real now and we were pushed on rapidly but cautiously.[2] When we reached Gainesville, about 10 A.M., the whole corps is excited and the rumour is circulated that the Yankee cavalry were

[1] This observation of Dooley's is interesting, though, it would seem, debatable. Jackson's position, now that Longstreet was so near, was relatively secure.

[2] Longstreet's march during the past three days had been remarkably swift. He had felt it necessary to push his men to the limit.

driven through this little place a few hours since by our advance.

The sun is intensely hot and we are jaded and parched with heat. Still we go on. Sounds of war are distinctly heard in front. We are told about midday[3] to load our guns, and this was my first loading with intent to *kill*. I had nearly forgotten about my last night's mishap and the rapid marching had taken the stiffness out of my limbs. I trembled with excitement and, I may add, with fear, for I was never *very* brave; and Capt. Mitchell had the kindness to give me some advice about loading and keeping cool when we should get under fire.

Here we go now, through the woods, deployed in line of battle;[4] about a half mile distant one of the enemy's batteries is posted looking for some antagonist, and our brigade is told to advance towards this terrible looking affair and afterwards to march by the right flank into some woods near by, and wait for further orders. Now we go right at them (as it were), they see us, and here come the shells crashing through the trees back of us and ploughing up the open field over which we are going. After marching until about 3 P.M. we passed over ground that the enemy had been driven from during the morning, and our Brigade was ordered again *to load*. Oh, how scared I felt! If I could only stay out of that fight with honor how gladly would I have done so! But I was today to smell gunpowder for the first time on a field of battle.

[3] This engagement of Aug. 29th, according to Dooley, began somewhat earlier than the accepted reports have led us to believe. If Dooley is correct, Longstreet showed less hesitation in precipitating the battle than has been commonly supposed.

[4] This engagement described by Dooley has been called the Battle of Groveton. It began with the clash between some reconnaissance forces of Hood and Evans and an advancing Federal column near that town. Pope was trying desperately to prevent the junction between Longstreet and Jackson.

Here we go thro' the woods, guns at a trail; now we deploy in line of battle in a field beyond; double quick—now across the railroad track—suffocating, nearly dead from the heat of the sun—now double quicking across a ploughed field, a fence right ahead and beyond that about 600 yds. a Yankee battery in full blast, belching forth flame, smoke, and bombshells, and worse than all, right at us. On, on, goes our line, right on as if we are going to charge those fearful engines of war. And how the shells scream and whistle, every one over our heads.

Close up forward—steady—dress to the right—give way on the left—don't crowd the center! And one of those enormous projectiles bursts immediately in front of the Regt., appearing to cover us all with dust. The two men beside me are knocked over and covered with dirt; though stunned, neither are hurt and on we go with the whining and whizzing and banging and a hundred contradictory orders [!] until we reach the fence afore mentioned, when we all lie down according to instructions, and await further developments. I was very much frightened and I am sure I wasn't the only one. Altho' the Yankees cannot see us in this position, yet they keep *a-feeling* for us, which is anything but pleasant, especially when a fellow reflects what *Sarching* things balls are.

Further developments having been made upon our left, our services can be dispensed with, and we are withdrawn for the evening[5] while Jackson, Hood, and others gain the

[5] This 'development on our left' was in reality a perilous set-back of the Confederate wing by Pope, who counter-attacked in an effort to free himself from the slowly-closing pincers of Longstreet and Jackson. We wonder, therefore, why Dooley's Brigade was 'dispensed with' and sent into reserve at this moment. Was this an example of Longstreet's caution, seeing that his men were so fatigued by their swift march under the hot sun? The situation on the Confederate left was saved by A. P. Hill and Maxcy Gregg's South Carolinians. Cf. Freeman, *op. cit.*, II, 221–224.

battle of Groveton. And I must confess I feel much safer and easier in mind and body while I listen to the volleys of musketry swelling in the distance, then becoming more distant until the out bursting of yells of our brave troops in the distance gives us assurance that all for us is well. Night closes around us, enveloping in a shroud of darkness the dead, the dying, and the sleeping armies.

SECOND MANASSAS

The next day, the memorable 30th of August, upon which we gained a complete victory over the boastful Pope, we rose betimes, and remained in line of battle all day until about 4 o'clock P.M., meanwhile the second battle of Manassas progressing furiously in our front and on our left.

About 4 P.M., when we had given up the idea of our being wanted today, one of Genl. Longstreet's aides came over the field as if life and death depended on his speed, as verily it did. How well the men knew what his presence indicated; and he had scarcely been recognized before they had each one regained his musket and were arranging themselves in order along the line. We had driven the Yankees back on the left and also on the right, and it was for Longstreet's fresh troops (ourselves) to press the center.[6]

[6] ". . . Longstreet had all his troops united and under the eye of Lee himself. Their position was one of exciting military interest. They were thrown diagonally across the Gainesville-Centreville Road in such a way that their line . . . formed an angle of about 160 degrees with Jackson's front. The two commands were jaws that opened widely to the Southeast. Would Pope be reckless enough to thrust his infantry arm into these jaws? Longstreet's men waited to see. . ." (Freeman, *op. cit.*, II, 121.) About 4 P.M. Jackson, his right being imperiled, asked Longstreet urgently for reinforcements. Longstreet's counter-attack (well-prepared by an artillery barrage) broke the Federal left and threw Pope's forces practically into a rout. This is the charge participated in by Dooley. He may be inaccurate in designating this Federal left flank the 'center'. Perhaps however it looked such to a soldier in the ranks of Longstreet's Brigades.

Success for Confederates

Here we go—closing up and double quick—now right in front marching by the flank so as to avoid the woods and other obstacles—now we are over a fence and the battery which we are to charge is right ahead. Again we form n line and now dashing thro' a cornfield; the bullets whistle thro' the leaves and ears and send many a brave comrade to his last account. But we have no time to think; such is the excitement, such the feeling with which I am inspired that I rush on with the rest, completely bewildered and scarcely heeding what takes place around.

And now the bullets strike the ground in front of us and comrades are falling pretty fast all around. I catch a glimpse of *the battery*; it's on a hill (quite a hill), and as we approach at a double quick all along the line the very earth seems to open and belch forth fire and smoke and balls. Back! down the hill! rolls the Brigade which had immediately preceded us; back! in utter rout and confusion, some shouting for us to *go back*—others to advance—some to *lie down*.

Still on we went double quick all the time right over the flying broken Brigade and up the hill—volley after volley—broadside after broadside comes crashing thro' our thinned ranks. Our Col., the brave old Skinner, on this day the bravest of the brave, 40 or 50 yds. ahead is cutting down the Yankee gunners who defend their pieces to the last.

'Fire!', rings out along the brigade, our muskets rattle out a volley along the whole line, and I find myself among dismounted cannon, broken caissons, bleeding horses, the dead and the dying.[7] Our gallant Col. (Skinner) comes reeling towards me bleeding profusely from three severe

[7] "We succeeded in driving the enemy from his line, near the Chinn House, capturing two batteries." (Loehr, *op. cit.*, p. 28).

wounds. 'Jack', said he, 'bear me witness that I was the first man on that battery'. 'I will, Col.', replied I, and I set to work to bind up the flow of blood which was streaming from his arm which was torn from wrist to elbow by a bullet. The Col. is soon carried from the field and I turn to look for the brigade which had in the mean time borne away to the left.[8]

The Yankees on the Run

I fall in with about 50 or 60 of ours who have become detached by that same leftward move. We all league together and drive thro' the woods a party of Yankees who keep up an annoying fire—and now we take possession of a rising knoll to the front and left where many of our men have gathered to play upon the advancing enemy. From this knoll, altho' constantly engaged, we have a splendid view of the Plain on our front and to the right. Some 500 or 600 yds. distant is a dense thicket or wood which must be filled by our troops. In front of this wood and directly in front of our position the whole plain, as far as the eye can reach, is covered with the blue of the enemy—some brigades flying in disorder, others advancing in serried lines with the Stars and Stripes innumerable floating in the breeze; officers vainly endeavoring to rally their wavering ranks furiously dashing up and down the lines.

Then little parties of flying soldiers [Federals] rallying

[8] There are some additional dramatic details to this incident of Colonel Skinner. It was his daughter Elsie who helped to bear him from the field of Second Manassas. She wrote later of ". . . our terrible ride, when we were taking him from the battlefield and were more afraid of a hemorrhage from the artery than of the Yankees, who were going from house to house, near Manassas, making prisoners of wounded officers." Skinner had actually killed with his sword three Yankee gunners, after receiving a bullet from each. He said, "I hated to kill those brave men. How splendidly they stood by their guns!" Cf. De Leon, *op. cit.*, 248–250.

are again and again led to the charge while our troops may be seen again and again on the advance; while their wild, fearful victorious yells give renewed confidence to us, strike terror to the souls of the Yankees and send them reeling back in disorder over the field. This appears to be their center, but a large portion of it is already in irremediable confusion; yet still the shell and bullets rain thick and fast around, and, as they speed along, sing and whistle the death song of hundreds of the fallen.

The Height of the Day's Fortunes

Oh, the horrid scenes around us! Brains, fractured skulls, broken arms and legs, and the human form mangled in every conceivable and inconceivable manner. And now the enemy seem gathering for fresh resistance—perhaps for an onset themselves by which they may hope to retrieve the fortune of the day and check our advance.

Yes! Here they come! Four or five lines of fresh troops deploy in the open plain in our front and direct their charge directly against that copse of woods off to our right. Oh, this is a splendid sight and one which the disinterested might well go in raptures over. Line after line of the best of the Yankee army steadily advances—and as orderly as if on parade; and it seems as tho' there was a slight cessation in the frightful roar of the artillery and musketry as these well drilled troops press on over the blood red plain.

At every step they take they see the piles of wounded and slain and their feet are slipping in the blood and brains of their comrades. Shells burst among them and a desultory musketry fire helps to thin their ranks; but still on they press, closing up steadily, splendidly. Many of their officers may be plainly distinguished riding beside their Brigades and Divisions, while the Stars and Stripes boastfully flaunt out defiance in the advance of each Regt.

Pope's Last Charge is Broken

On they come over dead and dying right at the copse of woods. The order is given, 'Charge!", and at a double quick the foremost lines charge against the woods. They are scarcely 50 or 80 yds. distant when a volume of smoke almost obscures the woods from our sight and volley after volley thunders against those ill fated columns. In vain does line after line advance at a run. Torn and bleeding they are hurled back, scattered, routed in confusion over the plain (blue with their slain.) In vain do their officers dash in the midst of this storm of shell and bullets. The fugitives will not be rallied, but, broken and dismayed, are pursued by our victorious troops until darkness closes around.

I was happy enough to witness this terrible slaughter and rout, but could not see the pursuit; for, Capt. Mitchell being wounded in the leg, Lt. Mercer and I bore him from the field; and as the enemy were now in complete rout and darkness was setting in, I remained with Capt. M. near the Corps Hospital while the wounded were being rapidly brought in.[9]

Upon the next day having buried our dead we moved forward on the track of the enemy.[10] On the 6th of September we were nearing the Potomac.

Today's (Sept. 6, 1862) marching is very fatiguing. I do not remember any march that so prostrated me as that of this first day of our invasion of the North. The sun is in-

[9] The Second Battle of Manassas had ended. Lee had severely damaged Pope's army, although he had not succeeded in his original plan of completely encircling it.

[10] The Confederate General-in-Chief now determined to push his advantage and continue his pursuit of the Federal forces into Maryland. This would be Lee's first large-scale invasion of Northern territory. September 6 found Longstreet's Division north of the Potomac and moving towards Buckeystown.

tensely warm and we are under its burning influence the whole day. When night shuts out the angry glare we are still marching slowly but wearily along the Maryland roads, sometimes half asleep, sometimes sound asleep [!]. Even when half asleep I moved for miles, my bruised, stiffened limbs mechanically following one the other. Sometimes I would drowsily wonder if it were possible for me to walk any further, if my feet would not refuse to make the very next step and in my own despite myself be compelled to halt. But I jogged along, dreaming in this way.

*At 2 A.M. on the morning of the 7th we crossed the Potomac and bivouacked near Buckeystown.[11]

I awoke on the morning of the 7th, little refreshed, and the first sight which struck my eye was Col. Corse[12] of Alexandria (who is in command of our brigade now, Gen. Kemper having charge of the division) at a little distance kneeling on *both* knees and most devoutly performing his morning orisons. Really his devout attitude before all his troops was giving much edification and would no doubt have spread much devotion and religion throughout the brigade. But suddenly his attention was diverted from his prayers to *meaner* things, and springing to his feet with all the energy of a little man and a brave and zealous officer, he hurled in quick succession the most ferocious invectives against a party of stragglers who were robbing a cornfield near by. 'You thieves, you robbers, you miserable skulking wretches etc.', he yelled, 'Sergeant, take a guard of men and arrest these rascally thieves; I'll teach them to rob the people in this style!'

[11] Dooley's pen seems here to have slipped. He must have meant the *evening of the 6th*, as is clear from what follows.

[12] Montgomery D. Corse, of Alexandria, Va. He was later promoted to Brigadier General. At the battle of Sharpsburg he was wounded for the third time.

Dooley Dissents

The Col. certainly did not lose sight of the temporal while attending to the spiritual, but although every one liked brave Col. Corse very much, still we didn't sympathize at all with him in the arrest of these so-called thieves, because our men having been witnesses of the devastation of fields through the entire State of Virginia, refused to understand why we should spare the fields of those who, if they were not actually hostile themselves, were supporting a hostile government.*

Once More on the March

About noon today, Sunday 7th, we move towards Frederick,[13] near which we arrive about 4 P.M. We bivouacked just at Monocacy Station on the bank of the river and close by the bridge which our men immediately began to prepare for destruction.—*Here we remained two days.

Interlude at Frederick

Ned Haines, our black servant boy who had made the campaigns of the 1st Manassas and the Peninsular with my Father and Brother, arrived bringing me letters, money, and other necessary articles, the most grateful of which was an excellent pair of shoes. These I needed more than anything else, and Ned declared himself forthwith ready to take care of me as he had done of my father before me.

While staying here I paid a visit to Frederick to look for some of my kind old Professors and Friends of Georgetown memory. As I approached the Novitiate[14] I met Fr. Paresce a few paces from the door, and although he had never

[13] While Jackson was moving up from Manassas northwestward and then northeastward to attack Harpers Ferry, Lee sent Longstreet around the Federal left wing towards Boonsboro to block any Federal retreat from Harpers Ferry. Frederick is on the road to Boonsboro.

[14] The elementary seminary of the Jesuits.

spoken to me but once before, he immediately recognized me, called me by name and invited me to come in. Here I was feasted and clothed anew. They insisted on supplying me with clean clothing, and indeed I needed underclothing as much as a poor dirty Confederate ever did. I bathed from head to foot and returned refreshed to camp, feeling clean all over. Perhaps I felt as if I too should be immured in those quiet halls; certainly it was my place, and if I was spared to reach it again after long weary wanderings, I might well exclaim, 'They have said Thy mercy, O Lord, is above all Thy works'.

Frederick Seems Lukewarm

There was a good deal of noise and cheering among our particular friends [as the Confederate troops passed thru Frederick] on this occasion; but it was not difficult to discern that this enthusiasm was roused only for the display, and that the large majority of the people were silent in regard to giving demonstrations of opinion; many because they were really hostile to us, and some because they knew that every one was narrowly watched by Spies, by the remnant of Yankee forces on parole in the town, and most of all by their own neighbors.

One of the War's Greatest Evils

This was one of the vilest evils produced and encouraged by our Civil War, that it often made the oldest and nearest neighbors the bitterest enemies and mutual spies. This most disgraceful evil, though not universal, might be found existing partially in every portion of our poor afflicted and invaded territory. It was not enough that grim visaged war swept with fire and sword through a defenceless country, that rich and abundant crops were wantonly ravaged and down trodden by a savage soldiery; that blooming fields and fragrant gardens, luscious orchards and verdant lawns withered and died like accursed things beneath the singeing flame of the lawless invaders; that hamlets and whole towns were plundered, their peoples outraged and the houses left masses of charred and smoking ruins; that through every portion of this devastated land the homesteads of the poor and the mansions of the rich were pillaged, fired and on their smoking ruins the most abominable and fiendish outrages perpetrated upon the poor defenceless women and children. . .

So many evils were not sufficient for the enemies of the Southern States, and for those foes of the human race, but there arose even amid such misery men and women who to curry favor with the invader pointed out their neighbors for still more dreadful punishments as being guilty of some special acts of disloyalty to that most enlightened and glorious government that the sun ever rejoiced to shine upon!

What the South Stood For

But there were many in Frederick bold enough to cheer as we passed, feeling that we were the last representatives of free government, and that when we fell the right of self government or the rights of States and peoples to govern themselves would fall with us; and despotism more galling than any tyranny of Europe would be forced upon the land by a party of brutal men, uneducated, unrefined, unprincipled, inhuman, criminal, and perjured.[15]*

I stopped today, *en passant*, at the Novitiate to bid the kind Fathers good-bye. Father Maguire is here and Jack Davis, an old class-mate. They are trying to get passports to carry him through to Baltimore. . . . Jack's entire senti-

[15] This is undoubtedly a severe judgment, but it is fair to say that it represents the typical Southern viewpoint at this time.

ments are Northern and he candidly told me so. I felt a little hurt, but endeavoured to shew myself as cordial towards him as he seemed to feel towards me, for I knew that his kind heart could never really beat in unison with those who had been so cruelly harassing our land. He wanted to do many things for me, and even tried to induce me to accept some of his clothing. Good-hearted Jack! I shall always remember your kindness and only wish that the infamous Yankee had no such brave heart among his degraded troops.

Father Ward Tries to be Diplomatic

Here too at the Novitiate were Yankee officers who have come to obtain Fr. Ward's (the Rector's) influence and credit in order that they may procure the necessary supplies of the townsfolk for their sick, wounded, and paroled soldiers who are here in garrison and hospital, having been captured upon the advent of our forces. Fr. Ward must be all to all and is equally polite to the Yankees and to myself. We are going, and they are coming; ah, much circumspection was necessary in those days, and even with the utmost care the man who was yielding in principle was doomed to suffer severely. . . .

We leave Frederick and move towards Boonsboro.[16] We

[16] On September 10 Longstreet resumed his march to Boonsboro, which lies on the west flank of South Mountain. According to the original orders he was to remain there, in order to intercept the expected retreat of the Federals from Harpers Ferry. Lee, however, fearing the approach of another Federal force advancing on Hagerstown from Pennsylvania, directed Longstreet not to pause at Boonsboro, but to leave D. H. Hill's force there and press on to Hagerstown in order to defend the valuable supply depot in that town. Longstreet made a forced march 13 miles through torrid heat to Hagerstown. On his arrival there, he found no trace of an approaching Federal army. Dooley is now describing this movement of September 10–13.

find the people of the countryside quite a contrast to the kind prodigality of their fields and orchards and the rich profusion of the same. They [the people] are as sour as vinegar; and it is generally the case in this part of Maryland and in similar parts of Pennsylvania that where the soil is richest and the produce most liberal, the cultivators are dried-up, cross-grained and mean.

Chapter Three

SOUTH MOUNTAIN AND SHARPSBURG

WE bivouacked tonight (Sept. 10) at the foot of South Mountain and the following day we proceeded leisurely over its summit. Passing through Boonsboro we bivouacked in the wood by a mountain stream, and the next day (Sept. 12), leaving Hagerstown on our right, we took possession of some woods between that town and Williamsport. In the meantime, Genl. Stonewall Jackson is on his way to capture Harpers Ferry, and most of our corps remain in this vicinity for the purpose of mutual support.[1]

The valley thro' which we had just passed was teeming with fertility in marked contrast with the barren fields of Virginia over which we had so recently trodden. Every where smiling fields of wheat, wide stretching acres of green corn with their yellow ears and crimson tassels met the eye; and on every hand were the pasture lands teeming with clover, timothy, and broad waving blades of nourishing grass; while every hundred yards extensive orchards, the branches of whose trees swept the ground with their luscious burdens of pears, peaches, and apples, invited the stragglers who flocked in numbers from each brigade, as it marched by, to gather into their pockets and havresacks the refreshing fruit.

Black Ned Shows His Loyalty

Ned, our black servant, went to Hagerstown early in the morning and brought back to me several bunches of

[1] Dooley seems to have been ignorant of the real purpose of Longstreet's march to Hagerstown. *Vide supra*, p. 29, note.

luscious grapes and other dainties. It seems he introduced himself into a respectable family and rendered himself popular not only with the servants but even with the mistress of the house, who, Ned declared, tried to induce him to desert the service and accept his freedom (which Uncle Sam was depriving his white progeny of and lavishly bestowing it on their blacks.)[2] 'But', said Ned, 'Massa John, they couldn't fool me. I knows too much about them abolishunists [sic]; they gets a feller to go 'long with 'em and then lets him shift for hisself, he! he! And then, Massa John', continued Ned, growing affected, 'it wouldn't do for me to leave you here in dat way, for if you gets wounded or anything happens to you, who going to take care about you and tell the folks at home when you are well?'

Moving into South Mountain

14th September. Early in the morning we are in line of march back to Boonsboro.[3] The preceding day we had passed quietly sleeping or amusing ourselves as best we could [in the Williamsport-Hagerstown area], whiling away the precious hours which should have been employed in rapid marching and in securing good positions for the coming battle.[4]

[2] This parenthesis is erased in the original Diary.

[3] Lee was becoming increasingly apprehensive of a Federal attack at Turners Gap, in South Mountain, about 2 miles southeast of Boonsboro. He therefore orders D. H. Hill to move from Boonsboro to the Gap, and directs Longstreet to march down from Hagerstown and join Hill. The latter's position is gravely imperiled by McClellan's interception of Lee's order, which reveals to the Federal commander that Hill is separated from Longstreet. The sequel was this: McClellan attacked Hill before Longstreet came up, and Hill was driven from his position in South Mountain. Longstreet, on his arrival, was likewise driven back.

[4] This interesting criticism by Dooley may be valid. Longstreet undoubtedly delayed in executing Lee's order to return to the Boonsboro-South Mountain area. Longstreet felt that both his own force and that

The enemy must be held in check at South Mountain until Jackson shall have surrounded and captured Harpers Ferry. The Yankees under McClellan have already with an army made up from every man that could be gathered in Maryland, Va., and Penna. attacked Gen. D. H. Hill in the Pass of South Mt. Hill has but a couple of brigades to hold in check an army of probably 130,000 men, ergo he must have reinforcement.

McClellan Wins A Point

The men speak in low meaning voices. A fight is no doubt expected, but no one knows anything for certain. We pass thru Hagerstown about 9½ A.M. while the church bells are ringing their warning sounds; and would that some warning bells had rung out for us yesterday and that we were where we are expected.

*It appears from after accounts that Gen. McClellan had been fortunate enough to capture or find despatches which explained the entire disposition of our forces; and finding that Gen. D. H. Hill of N.C. had but one division guarding South Mountain, and only a very small body of men at Crampton Gap, had determined like a good and watchful General, to catch us napping; and throwing the entire weight of his army (one hundred thousand strong, at the very least) upon this small division, crush it before the rest of our army could come to its support.

How he succeeded the sequel proves. My remembrance of it is that he first attacked upon Saturday evening,[5] pushing forward his divisions one after another as they left

of D. H. Hill should fall back to Sharpsburg. It is possible, as Dooley says, that if Longstreet had started back to Boonsboro sooner than the morning of the 14th, he and Hill might have been able to secure more advantageous positions on South Mountain.

[5] September 13.

Frederick and Middletown, in quick succession, until by Sunday noon he had massed nearly his entire army on South Mountain, gradually driving D. H. Hill back from point to point until by 8 P.M. the passes were untenable by us. Of course as soon as Genl. Lee was apprised of the imminent danger of D. H. Hill at South Mountain, he hurried forward as fast as possible all his available troops. We had only two corps d'armée, Jackson's and Longstreet's. Jackson's was at Harpers Ferry, and our corps was all that could be opposed to the enemy.* But even with these odds, had we taken position last evening before the heights were gained, the enemy could never have wrested so strong a position from us. Nay, Gen. McClellan was too good a general even to have attempted it.

Longstreet Tries to Come to the Rescue

As we advance[6] on the Hagerstown road [towards Boonsboro] we hear now and then fresh rumours of the fight. Severe fighting is going on ahead, and the impression is that our troops are being hard pressed. Our pace quickens and the roar of the cannon is distinctly heard.

About two o'clock P.M. we pass through Boonsboro[7] and soon an ambulance goes by containing the remains of Gen. Garland of Lynchburg, former Col. of the 11th Va. of our Brigade. He was killed this morning, and we are told that it was on account of the desperate condition of our affairs in the mountain. Gen. Lee is near by, and he too is in an

[6] This was on September 14.

[7] "Word had come that Longstreet's troops were nearing Boonsborough. Hill's answer was a request that 'Old Pete' hurry. As the Federals seemed to be massing rapidly, Hill was anxious to assail them on his reinforced right [i.e. reinforced by Longstreet] before they delivered their major blow, which he thought was apt to come on his left." (Freeman, *op. cit.*, II, 180.)

ambulance. His arm is in a sling and it would appear that he too is wounded. These two mishaps make us feel pretty gloomy. (Gen. Lee's accident had occurred when his arm had been sprained by being thrown from his horse.)

The Retreat at South Mountain

Upon the spurs to our right and even a little to our rear the enemy have succeeded in gaining strong positions, and as we attempt to ascend the steepest portion of the road, which passes over the summit, we come in full view and under complete range of their guns. It is now about 5 o'clock and the shells of the enemy come whistling over our heads fast and furiously as we ascend the mountain.

Troops of the most demoralized stragglers are descending as we ascend, and long lines of wounded limping down the road. The appearances of things are to say the least very discouraging. Scarcely are we at the summit or near the summit than a battery but a short distance away opens ball and shell upon our ranks from a spur of the mount nearly opposite, and as it sweeps every yard of the road over which we are passing the greatest confusion for a time prevails. There is no commanding officer, no orders of any kind have been given to the Brigade; we are marching by the flank and not a musket is loaded. In the midst of this confusion, crash and roar of the artillery, Capt. Becker of Genl. Kemper's staff, than a braver young man never lived, undertook to lead us where we would escape the terrible fire and meet the Yankee infantry on open ground.[8]

'Shells Bursting in Air'

I tell you, I was frightened! These balls (round shot) not content with making the ordinary scare, bounding over

[8] "We were placed in position on the hill to the left of the turnpike, where we engaged the enemy" (Loehr, *op. cit.*, 30.)

and above and around and among us, go crashing into the crags on our left, splintering into a thousand pieces large fragments of rock which wildly fly around our heads, and the crash resounding from ridge to ridge multiplies indefinitely the fearful reports and increases very much the terror which such missiles are wont to inspire. One shot went through a tree about three feet in diameter, splitting nothing but leaving a nice round smooth hole in the body. Another shot (I thought I saw it then) came bounding along the mountain side and right through our regiment. What a scatteration it made! John Daniels of Co. H was the only one hit.

The Confederates Brace Temporarily

Over the fence now, and straight in front we are to find the enemy. Not a gun has been loaded, so suddenly and hastily have we been brought into action. Here under this terrible fire of artillery, creating more terror than havoc, we load our muskets and the regiment is pushed forward to the edge of a field to the right of the road and on the brow of the mountain. Before us the field and fences and sides of the mountains swarm with Yankees, triumphant in their success, but cautious in their advance.

Too Late!

The victory is theirs; in fact, long before we arrived, the most important points had been carried, and all that remained was to check this tide of triumphant blue coats and secure a safe retreat. Of course our Brigade was not the only one to assist in this, but I speak principally of our action because we knew little of what others were doing when we ourselves were engaged.

The enemy's forces are elated and are determined to

carry everything before them this evening, and are not long in attacking our line. Our men behave very well but we are too few and the blue coats are very many. Our Brigade is sent to defend a position or line which a whole Brigade might be supposed able to protect. Our Brigade should have about four thousand men to do the duty required of it and has at the very highest calculation no more than 400, ten times less than its complement.

There was not a fair fight here, and the bullets got so entirely *pranky*, *disorderly*, and *murderous* in their intent that although our brave fellows behave well and pay back with interest whatever favours were intended for them, still after about an hour and a half of retreating from position to position the Brigade gave it up as a hopeless business, and came back over the brow of the mountain even faster than they went up. Here those execrable batteries open on us again to complete our discomfiture. But they did not succeed; for we rally again and although things are pretty much confused we form a good line lying on our faces while shell and shot and bullet screamed and whistled over our heads.

John Dooley's Pride Has a Close Call

My idea was that this position was growing intensely warm, and I considered it a great want of prudence on our part to remain. In fact, nothing but pride, sense of duty and shame of hurting my reputation kept me in this awful state of suspense. Before we rallied upon the side of the mountain I was just making up my mind to make a double quick *change of direction* to the base of these heights, when a Capt. Mitchell of the 11th Va., who was doing all he could to rally the Brigade, clapped me on the back, saying, 'Hurrah for you! You are one of the 1st Va. I know you'll stand by us to the last!' What could I do under such circumstances?

Was I to run and prove myself a coward? No Sir! So I just laid down with the others who were making a last *stand*, lying.

So Ends The Battle of South Mountain

The enemy cheered and hurrahed—they never *shouted* like our men, but gave three *cheers methodically*, and by Regiment or Brigade—and oh, how the bullets whistled over our heads! But the blue coats were too cautious to come to the crest of the mountain behind which we were in ambush, and now dark having set in, the infantry slackened their fire. There is a lull in the battle during the night.

Withdrawal Through Boonsboro

*About 11 P.M. the remnant of our little army began its retreat in silence, so silently that according to their own account the enemy knew nothing of it until the next morning (the 15th) when even our rear guard was out of danger. All talk in a low tone of voice and the movement of their canteens as they knock against their legs and hips are the only sounds to be distinguished. Our turn comes soon [i.e. the turn of Dooley's regiment] and we, probably about two hundred, move quietly and wearily along. We had been marching and fighting all day and must now march and probably fight all night. Captain Norton's company is reduced to *two members*, an *officer* and a *private;* that is, *himself* and *myself*.

Aftermath of Battle

Half through Boonsboro and then turn to the left. Hundreds of our wounded are gathered in this little village, crowding the porches and steps of the houses and begging admittance; and we hear many voices from the various windows telling these poor victims of war to go away and not to get *them* (the inmates) into trouble. They are opposed to us all along this valley, and are or pretend to be fearful of punishment from the Yankees if they befriend us in any way. Guards and patrols are stationed at the turning and at intervals along the road to guide the march and prevent straggling into the fields off the road, also to bring forward those lagging behind.

Lee and Longstreet Take Position at Sharpsburg

After limping on for about half a mile, we come up with the rear guard who warn us to move on ahead as fast as possible, for the enemy's cavalry are very close in pursuit and are expected to attack every moment. Our Brigade which in the coming battle of Antietam was to occupy almost the extreme right of the line, moves on for about two miles or more and rests upon a hill side close by the little town of Sharpsburg.[9] Here with many other brigades we remained until late in the noon. Orders were then given for us to march through an orchard on the outskirts of the town and take up a position upon a hill close by the little town of Sharpsburg.[10*]

[9] "Lee's withdrawal of Longstreet and of D. H. Hill from South Mountain, after the news of the impending capture of Harpers Ferry, had been directed to Sharpsburg for three reasons: at that point, Lee would be on the flank and potentially in rear of McClellan in the event the Federal commander sought to cut off McLaws [who was marching in a northeasterly direction above Sharpsburg]; second, Sharpsburg was close to the Potomac across which the forces under Jackson were to move to reunite with Lee; third, the terrain around Sharpsburg was moderately favorable for defensive action, though the position was not as deep as Lee would have desired. Antietam Creek itself, running North and South, was scant protection. Across it were four bridges in addition to several fords which, though difficult, were by no means impassable." (Freeman, *op. cit.*, II, 203.)

[10] "Once arrived at Sharpsburg, the two infantry divisions were disposed along the high ground to cover the Boonsborough road, by which they had marched, and the road from Hagerstown, fourteen miles to the North. For the protection of these roads and for the defence of the ridges,

September 15. Today Jackson, the Great Stonewall of our army, has with the brilliancy of Napoleon the 1st captured the large garrison of Harpers Ferry, stores, munitions, etc. and is now on his march to assist the hard pressed attenuated corps of Longstreet. A place on the left has been kept for him where his unconquered veterans are again to hurl back in discomfiture and slaughter the unnumbered legions of the enemy.[11]

McClellan Probes the Confederate Lines

Sept. 16th. The left of our line was the first point attacked, to test our strength, and the principal efforts of the enemy will be directed against the left wing in order to turn our flank and intervene between our army and the Potomac.[12] Such was the admirable nature of the ground chosen by Lee that the enemy was engaged till late in the afternoon in reconnoitering our position, and before he had completed his observations Stonewall Jackson reached the field from Harpers Ferry and with more than half his corps met the first movements of the Yankee army on our left.

McClellan Opens His Barrage

In the mean time about 10 A.M. the artillery of the enemy opened a furious cannonade upon our lines, center

---

the Confederate Army was alarmingly weak in comparison with an adversary who followed fast and boldly deployed. Even after Jackson arrived on the 16th and took position on the left, the Army was weaker than ever it had been under Lee. The full effects of straggling and of dispersion of force were plain for every soldier to see. A strong attack by the whole of McClellan's command manifestly would threaten not merely defeat but ruin. The worst of all the succession of crises had come. An army of liberation was an army in desperation." (Freeman, *op. cit.*, II, 203–204.)

[11] Rather too optimistic!

[12] McClellan sent one of Hooker's corps against Jackson and Hood, stationed just south of the West Wood. This was a mere 'feeling out' operation, a skirmish preliminary to the main battle of the morrow.

and right, but principally upon the town of Sharpsburg in the rear and a little to the right of the center. Our Brigade and other troops are posted in front of the town, we being a little to the right. We are posted behind the crests of elevated ground extending for some distance on our right and left. By care and circumspection we are able to conceal the movements of our army almost entirely from the enemy, and the wild firing of their gunners today shews conclusively that they are ignorant of our positions. Not knowing where to throw their shells, they took Sharpsburg for the object of their aim, and for nearly half the day shell and shot rained continually upon this devoted little town.

This was a grand and fearful spectacle, and to me, who had never seen any continuous cannonading, it was perfectly thrilling. The men around me said it was the severest shelling they had ever witnessed. We were between the enemy and this town, and though they could not see us, I felt afraid that they would soon find us out and that took away much of the pleasure that the bombardment would otherwise have afforded me.

Every shell went screaming, whistling, whining over our heads, and not a few burst near by us. Sometimes shell after shell would burst in quick succession over the village and we did not know whence they came or how they got there. None of our soldiers were in the town, except the cooks and a few stragglers who hid themselves in the cellars as soon as the bombardment began, and told us afterwards of the wonderful escapes they made from 'them bursting lamp-posts.'

The shelling ceased in the afternoon and an attack was made upon our left which Gen. Jackson repulsed;[13] and

[13] Dooley is repeating what he has already said above (p. 40.) Jackson repulsed (on the 16th) Hooker's probing movement against the Confederate left south of the West Wood.

his men, according to many reports, slept almost feet to feet with their own men, ready to begin the fight as soon as there was light enough to discern friend from foe. (Imagine men sleeping within a few yards of each other and about to kill one another at the slightest warning!) *We* rested quietly, having no fear of immediate danger and making the best of the little respite afforded us.

Opposing Objectives and Relative Strengths

*Wednesday Sept. 17th was a day that will not be easily forgotten by those who participated in the sanguinary battle of Antietam or Sharpsburg. It was the object of the enemy to drive us from the Sharpsburg and Potomac road along which our line for a good distance was extended. Our object was to repel all assaults upon the road by which we were to retreat into Virginia. We were unable to attack since our army consisted of less than 30,000 men all told, part of whom were broken down and bare footed, all of whom were wearied troops who were about to close a campaign of the severest fighting and most fatiguing marches the world had ever heard of, no matter in what clime or time. On the other hand, the Yankee general opposed to our immortal Lee had, according to the journals of the North, 100,000 men more than we had, of which more than 60,000 or 70,000 were fresh troops who had not struck a blow during the campaign. Such were some of the odds against us on this glorious day.

Our army called this battle by the name of Sharpsburg because our center rested nearly upon the little town bearing this name, and because it was from this position that the enemy put forth all their strength to expel us, and failed despite the utmost efforts. The Yankees have given the name of 'Antietam' to the contest, because along the little stream of that name their army was deployed, and across it they had to come in order to attack. But as we came nearer driving them from their position than they did in regard to us (I speak especially of their right wing), they give the name of Antietam to imply thereby that they had repulsed us from their position rather than that we had repelled them with terrible slaughter from ours.

As early as the dawn of the 17th our left wing and the enemy's right became hotly engaged.[14] According to their own account (Hist. of Penna. Reserve Corps)—for I have not seen our own—after a pretty sharp resistance our first line gave way and fled to the woods in our rear, bordering the Hagerstown pike. On reaching these woods, the dense mass of pursuers were hurled back in confusion over half the ground they had taken, by fresh bodies of Rebels;[15] and the carnage was so great, say they, that Divisions[16] retreated back not larger than Brigades, and Brigades were diminished to Regiments.

Jackson Sets the Trap

Here[17] was the severest and deadliest struggle of the day. 4 times they took possession of this *trap*, and as often were repulsed with ample carnage. And towards noon, their accounts tell us, that had not the Rebels been too much weakened themselves, the grand Union army would have

[14] Hooker again attacked Jackson's positions at the south end of the West Wood, and forced a partial Confederate withdrawal. Jackson at once called on Hood, Early, and D. H. Hill for reinforcements.

[15] Hood, Early, and D. H. Hill succeed in manoeuvering Hooker into a pocket,—the 'trap' described by Dooley in the next paragraph. Hooker's first attempt to break through is repulsed.

[16] i.e., Federal Divisions.

[17] Hooker repeated his vicious attacks three times, but was finally stopped in his tracks, at least temporarily. Jackson's position was for the moment secure; but the cost to the Confederates in killed and wounded had been terribly high.

found itself in danger of annihilation.[18] Here were at least 60,000 massed against less than 20,000, and only saved from disaster and utter defeat by the losses of the enemy, that is, ourselves. It was at this time that news was brought to our right,[19] that Jackson's gallant little army was driving the enemy before them and victory would crown his efforts.*

The Attack Now Shifts to the Confederate Center

About 11 A.M. (I think) the enemy advanced upon our center. We have a good view of our batteries, and as line after line of the blue coats advance to the charge, our guns open at about two hundred yards' distance and the grape mows them down like wheat before the scythe.[20] We can plainly see the earth as it is torn up and scattered wildly about in face of each successive line of infantry that marches up the slope; for the enemy must march up a slight acclivity before they see the battery or can themselves be seen. No ammunition appears to be wasted and not a shot is fired by us until the enemy line appears on the crest of the elevation; and then every gun opens almost simultaneously and back go the flying Union troops pell-mell, leaving bloody traces of their disorderly retreat.

This was the finest sight we witnessed today. Time and again fresh battalions were advanced against these central batteries but no line got nearer than two hundred yards,

[18] Had the Union army been really placed in such a predicament at this stage of the battle?

[19] i.e. to Longstreet's Divisions and Dooley's regiment; what Dooley terms the Confederate right had taken no active part in the engagement thus far.

[20] Dooley's account of the Federal attack against the Confederate center would appear to be marked by a *pro patria* bias. The fact is that by noon the Federals had practically wrecked the Confederate center, forcing Rodes to withdraw his troops. Cf. Freeman, *op. cit.*, II, 210–217.

and all were hurled back from the top of the hillock as regularly as they came to the charge. This was all done by grape shot, no musketry as far as we could see being used at all at this point.

Dooley Moves Into Action

It is now noon, and we who have hitherto been inactive spectators of this scene must take our part, though small, in the action. Burnside's corps is moving against our position, the contest having extended from left to right.[21] We are moved to meet this attack almost between the advancing enemy and the town of Sharpsburg. A few of our men are in the orchard afore mentioned, and behind a stone wall, and the majority behind a rail fence on the borders of a cornfield. Two pieces of artillery are all that can be spared to keep the enemy back, and these are but very poor guns.

A Critical Position

I might very readily omit what follows as reflecting but little credit on our gallant old brigade; but as I think it reflects no disgrace I shall tell the whole truth. When ordered into position to meet the enemy our brigade was again supposed to be able to do the duty of a full brigade or at least to try to do it. So depleted was it however that our Regt. had but 17 men rank and file, 8 officers and 9 men. With this brigade of about 200 men we covered a space of nearly as many yards, not presenting a skirmish line.

The Yankees Drive Nearer!

In the field below us the enemy are slowly but cautiously approaching, crouching low as they advance behind the

[21] As a matter of fact the Confederate right (where Dooley was) was being threatened with ruin. The movement now being described by Dooley was a counter-attack ordered by Lee in a desperate effort to save the situation. This counter-attack failed, and the Confederates broke and ran, as Dooley relates.

undulating tracks in the rich meadows through which they are passing. From the numbers of their flags which are distinctly visible above the rising ground we judge them to be at least two thousand in number. As long as our little battery of two guns is served with tolerable precision the enemy, who appear to be new troops, do not dare to venture close or raise their heads. But in a few minutes the Yankee artillery, far superior to ours, dismounted one of our pieces, killed the horses; and the remaining gunner, fearing capture, hitched the only remaining horse to the other cannon and made away to the rear as hard as he could go.

I shall never forget poor Beckham on Kemper's staff. As soon as our first gun opened on the enemy, he gave a lusty cheer and rising in his stirrups flung his hat around his head, wild with enthusiasm. Almost instantly he was hurled from his horse by a shot and his foot terribly mangled. He was borne from the field cheering as he went and with him went General Kemper and his staff.

John Dooley Runs

We were now left to oppose the numerous masses before us with a mere picket-line of musketry. There may have been other troops to our left and right but I did not see any. The Yankees, finding no batteries opposing them, approach closer and closer, cowering down as near to the ground as possible, while we keep up a pretty warm fire by file upon them as they advance. Now they are at the last elevation of rising ground and whenever a head is raised we fire. Now they rise up and make a charge for our fence. Hastily emptying our muskets into their lines, we fled back through the cornfield.

Oh, how I ran! or tried to run through the high corn, for my heavy belt and cartridge box and musket kept me back to *half* my speed. I was afraid of being struck in the *back*, and I frequently turned half around in running, so as to avoid if possible so disgraceful a wound. It never entered my head to throw away gun or cartridge box; but, encumbered as I was, I endeavored to keep pace with my captain, who with his long legs and unencumbered would in a little while have far outstripped me but that he frequently turned towards the enemy, and, running backwards, managed not to come out ahead in this our anything but creditable race. The enemy having taken our position appeared to think they had performed wonders, for instead of pursuing us and shooting us down, they began to give regular *methodical* cheers, as if they had gained a game of base ball.

The Retreat Halted by Toombs' Georgians

Scarcely had we, breathless, reached the edge of the cornfield than we met Toombs' brigade of Georgians advancing in line of battle to our relief. Hastily forming in their rear we returned to our former line which by this time a well directed volley from this little brigade of Georgians had restored again to our possession. Still, even with this brigade, we were scarcely 800 men, and how were we to repulse the thousands that still threatened us, backed as they were by a terribly efficient artillery force?

General Toombs rides up and down the line like one frantic, telling the men to stand firm, etc., and sends off for reinforcements of artillery. In less than ten minutes two pieces of the Washington Artillery are hurried rapidly forward to our support. They choose a pretty position, far safer and more advantageous than that of the other battery, and in a few minutes are playing with wonderful effect on the cowering lines of the enemy.

It was astonishing to witness the rapidity and coolness of these comrades, and with what admirable tact and skill they managed their pieces. Not once during the whole evening did they suffer disaster to their guns, whilst they together with our small force of infantry (Georgians and Virginians) kept the enemy cowering in the meadows beyond us until the darkness of night shrouded the field and its carnage from our sight, and both armies slept on their arms amid the dead and the dying, amid the havoc and debris of the red field of battle.

A Summary

*Thus ended the battle of Antietam. The troops opposite to us were certainly no paragons of bravery, for they should have been able to crush our puny little force and destroy entirely our right wing. The enemy had (according to Northern reports) with 90,000 men tried from day break until night to force back from its position our barefoot, ill-rationed, jaded army, short of ammunition and scarcely amounting to 30,000 muskets; and, after tremendous losses which he himself acknowledged, ten or twelve of his generals being killed or wounded, his only boast is that he preserves *his* line on the Antietam unbroken and that our glorious little army, acting *purely* on the defensive, *had not been able* to drive him across the stream, which now gives its name to the battle.[22]

We have not receded one inch from left to right or yielded a single position that we held in the morning. Gen. Lee in his official report acknowledges to have had about 36,000 men. Of course he ought to know, but I doubt very much that he had had 36,000 men ready for action, because there

[22] Despite Dooley's attempt to put the best face on a bad situation the fact remains that the Confederate invasion of Maryland had been stopped cold. Admitting, for the sake of argument, that the Confederates had won a tactical victory (to some extent) at Antietam, they had certainly been defeated from the larger strategical viewpoint.

were numbers who were reported on the *rolls*, who on account of being barefoot and stragglers, did not engage in the battle.[23]

The fact is I believe that our army was in a more deplorable condition than any one except the individual soldiers were willing to admit. At one time during the heat of the day when the enemy were pressing on our batteries with fearful odds, Gen. Longstreet rode up to some guns (the same, I think, that we had witnessed so triumphantly repelling the enemy from our center) which were almost completely unmanned; and bidding his whole staff dismount they worked these guns with their own hands until the enemy, wearied and disheartened by the carnage in his ranks, withdrew and turned fresh columns upon our right.*

The Day After the Battle

Sept. 18th, 1862. This morning we occupy the same ground as yesterday and anxiously look for a renewal of yesterday's assault from the enemy. Well might we fear, with only the skeleton of an army, the heavy masses of blue coats in our front. But the position chosen by our noble Lee was so admirably suited for a successful defence, that he had determined to remain and deliver a second battle if necessary. To attack the enemy would have been madness, although Gen. Lee in appealing to some of our barefoot stragglers urged them to rejoin their regiments in order to make a strenuous effort to drive the enemy across the Antietam. Of course he wished to put confidence in their

[23] Freeman, *op. cit.*, II, 225, thus summarizes the relative losses in the campaign of invasion: "The price of the expedition had been for the Confederates 13,609 casualties or more. Of these, about 10,000 represented Sharpsburg. Federal losses were 27,767, of which Harpers Ferry accounted for 45 per cent. Twice as many men the Federals had lost as had the Confederates, but one for two was more than the South could afford to pay."

demoralized hearts. However, we kept on our hills in quiet possession of the Battlefield.

Little Reward for Charity

During the morning I was sent to the town to bring back any stragglers that I might find; but not meeting any I returned to the Brigade. All our wounded have been conveyed to safe field hospitals; but there are a large number of wounded Yankees about twenty, thirty, and forty yards in our front that wished to be removed; and details of ours are endeavoring to bring them in. But so dangerous and incessant a fire is kept up by the enemy's Sharpshooters that it is a very hazardous enterprise to go beyond our lines. Nevertheless our *barbarous soldiers* are employed in this humane undertaking and have brought in several of these wretches when one member of the 7th Va. Inf. is struck in the heart by a Minnie ball and expires in a few minutes. This sad event put a stop to any humanity or charitable movements towards the enemy's wounded, since they would rather see their own men die than refrain from the pleasure of killing ours.

All day long we remain quietly in front of Sharpsburg,[24] and the enemy are just as quiet, save their murderous sharpshooters who are continually on the 'qui vive' to 'hurt some body'. About night fall orders from Headquarters come to the brigade that we must resume as quietly as possible our retreat towards the Potomac at 11 P.M.

We take advantage of the few hours left us and enjoy quite a refreshing nap, until we are awakened by the bustle around us; and, folding up our blankets, strapping on our cartridge boxes and shouldering our muskets, we are on

[24] Lee apparently was willing to risk another day's fight at Antietam if the Federals should make the attack. On the 18th, however, he heeded the dictates of caution and began his uncontested retreat to the south shore of the Potomac.

our way back to Va. The retreat is conducted with the utmost order and caution.

Comic Relief at Sharpsburg

We have to rest for about ten or fifteen minutes in Sharpsburg, and while waiting, as usual, one of the men took about a dozen canteens of the more lazy fellows to fill them with water. This man, McCrossin, was fond of a practical joke, and being absent a little longer than the obtaining water warranted we wondered what was detaining him. Just as we were moving on he comes back and hastily delivered the canteens to their owners. I am very thirsty and take a good draught from my canteen immediately; it was nothing but strong raw whiskey. I went to several other canteens asking for water, and all I came to had whiskey in them. It appears that McCrossin had filled the canteens from a whiskey barrel instead of from a spring; and he was the boy to know if there were any strong whiskey barrels about town, with no one in particular to claim them. We easily obtained water for whiskey.

Vignette of Lee

About 7 o'clock in the morning we crossed the Potomac, with Gen. Lee close by the river bank, mounted and motionless as the night itself. Few reflect upon the anxiety which fills the breast of such a man upon an occasion when the lives and safety of so many depend on his will and direction.

The Doubtful Slaughter at Boteler's Ford

About day break, Sept. 19th, we halt for an hour.[25] The whole army has crossed and the enemy are only beginning

[25] Note that Freeman, following the sources, places this so-called 'bloody repulse' of the Federal force on the morning of the 20th. Cf. *op. cit.*, II, 233.

their pursuit. About nine o'clock their advance guard arrives, and soon after begin their crossing. Never was anything more foolishly attempted. A. P. Hill's Division of Infantry advanced to the bluff overhanging the river, and concealing themselves until the Yankees reached the middle of the stream, poured into this dense mass of human beings volley after volley, until the whole river was filled with floating corpses and wounded, drowning men.[26]

The artillery, too, posted in advantageous positions, played on this floating mass until there were but few left to bear back the tidings of defeat and slaughter. Enough however was seen by the army behind, to prevent any pursuit during the day. Of this terrible affair the Yankees make no mention at all. But Genl. Jackson in his official report declares that he never witnessed 'greater slaughter, the river being perfectly blue with the bodies of the dead and drowning'.

[26] This description by Dooley of the repulse of the Federals at Boteler's Ford is contradicted by Freeman's more accurate account, which runs as follows: "Pendleton was given orders by Lee to prevent the Federals from crossing the Potomac at Boteler's Ford. . . . Some of the Federals got across on the night of the 19th-20th, and captured some of Pendleton's artillery. Learning of the repulse, Jackson, by 6:30 A.M. on the 20th, had ordered A. P. Hill to return to the Potomac and to drive the enemy back across it. This was done by Hill. A frightful slaughter it seemed, but actually the Federal losses were not heavy, because the force was not large. . ." (Freeman, *op. cit.*, II, 233.) It is interesting to note that Lee himself (according to Dooley) seems to have exaggerated the importance of the 'victory'. Dooley's view of the action was doubtless shared by the typical Confederate soldier in the ranks.

CHAPTER FOUR

INTERLUDE IN CAMP

DURING the day we lounged around the woods and fields awaiting the approach of the enemy from several directions. But in the afternoon, finding nothing to do we marched several miles towards Martinsburg, and bivouacked for the night.* We remained several days near Martinsburg, resting and watching the movements of the enemy. Leaving the vicinity of Martinsburg we came by easy marches to the neighbourhood of Winchester. Here we were destined to stay for three or four weeks, resting from our labors, recruiting our depleted ranks, and renewing our discipline which had sorely suffered during our long and arduous campaign.

Gen. Lee issued an order here in which, reviewing all that his little army had done during the past summer, he passed the highest encomiums upon his soldiers for their courage, endurance, and perseverance and success.

HAZLITT AND AN UNHYGIENIC LIEUTENANT

I amused myself while here for several days with a book called 'Table Talk' by Wm. Hazlitt; and Lieut. Cabell of Co. H came over frequently during the day to see me. Lieut. C. took a kind of pride in keeping himself unclean, and I often thought he did it from principle, seeing that he never took advantage of any occasion that offered of making himself appear cleaner. Though a slow speaker he is a man of good education, and, so far as I could judge, a man of good natural talents. We sit in company for hours discussing Mr. Hazlitt's book and many other interesting topics. He wears a heavy overcoat morning, noon, and evening, and at night, nor do I know why, unless it is for the better protection of the houseless wanderers (vermin) that are beginning to infest our camps in overwhelming numbers.

Speaking of Gallantry—

C. has much experience in many things and we pass many pleasant hours together. Among other things he told me that after the late battle of Antietam he overtook one of our soldiers on the road whistling very cheerfully and marching briskly towards Old Virginia. When C. came close to him he was amazed to discover that this poor soldier's arm had been shot off and was connected with the elbow only by a piece of skin. The gallant hero was bearing his arm along with him, having slung it over his shoulder just as he would his gun. Whistling right merrily he was glad enough to escape at any cost from the Yankees' clutches and would brave all sufferings to keep up with the army.*

Entertainment, Religious and Otherwise

The ministers (chaplains) of the different regiments are now on the 'qui vive' (Alert), and prayer meetings and preaching are beginning to be quite common. Every evening before dusk the chaplains begin preaching, and for miles around you might hear thousands of voices singing hymns; many singing for their own gratification, but many others through a *sort* of religious feeling of their own, thinking that this is the most convenient way of manifesting it. After they get tired, Bill Dean[1] of Co. G opens his *opera*, and

[1] Sergeant William H. Dean died a prisoner of war at Point Lookout.

his vocal troupe make the woods resound with such glee songs as 'Nelly was a lady', 'Come to de ol' gum tree', 'Give me a hut', 'Sound, sound de banjo', etc., until the nightly tatoo bids all vocal sounds to cease and the nocturnal chorus of forest insects and the distant croaking of frogs lull the soldier to rest on his grassy couch.

Psychology of Leadership by Lee

We amuse ourselves often by telling incidents of the past campaign. I heard a good one about Gen. Lee.

The morning after the battle of Sharpsburg Gen. Lee was riding by a hay stack some hundred yards in the rear of the battle line and observed two or three of our regt. snugly esconced in a hay pile. 'My good men', cried he, 'what Regt. do you belong to?' They, frightened and blushing, full of shame, shewed him their swollen and bleeding feet, telling him that it was impossible to keep up with the marches of the Regt., and that they were members of the 1st Va. Infantry. 'What!' cried our noble General, 'members of the glorious 1st! The first Regiment that Virginia placed in the field and which has never yet proved recreant to its duty! No, no; rise, my good fellows and rejoin your Regiment, for we must make another effort today to drive these people across the Antietam!' Our brave fellows did rejoin us and told us they were never so ashamed in their lives as when the Noble old General exhorted them so kindly and feelingly to renewed efforts of courage and endurance.

(Hundreds of those who participated in the battle were faint thru want of food and maimed with cut and swollen feet. But thousands and tens of thousands were stragglers, scattered and hopeless burdens upon the farmers of Northern Virginia.)

A Good Rest and Pats on the Back

We have now settled down for a good rest and indeed we need it. The manifesto[2] of Gen. Lee, great, noble, kind hearted Gen. Lee, has cheered us much. He set forth in feeling words his admiration of our heroism and endurance. He reviewed the past campaigns from Mechanicsville to Sharpsburg and without the slightest exaggeration made every man of us a hero, adorned us with the laurels of victory and filled our hearts with exuberant joy to think and to know that we have fulfilled the highest expectations and met with the highest approbation of our Beloved Leader. For who does not love Gen. Lee, who would not barter life for his smile? And now that he speaks in words of love and admiration to his wearied troops, who does not feel every syllable burning in his very heart's core?

Relax, Soldier

Let us pause now and stretch our weary limbs upon the grass plots or falling leaves of our Bivouack. We are getting our regular rations now, boiled beef and pones of wheaten bread. You may also by good management continue to purchase extras at a neighbouring farmhouse, but provisions are very scarce and it is not often the people have anything to sell.

Ned Haines Stays On

Ned Haines, my colored boy, is still with me, having remained faithful during the whole campaign, and there was nothing to prevent him from going to the Yankees had he such an idea, for I didn't see him for more than a week while in Maryland. But Ned appears to have an idea that were he to go away I should be utterly at a loss how to get on without him. Perhaps he has his own difficulties also,

[2] This has already been mentioned by Dooley. *Vide supra*, p. 53.

for Ned, like all negroes, would not like to labour for his living.

A (Temporarily) Quiet Life

Sometimes I roam the fields and watch the sinking sun gilding the bright or sombre hues of the autumnal forests with expiring rays, or watch the ragged veterans returning from the Springs, ladened with canteens of cool sparkling water, good humour in their eyes and ragged homespun on their limbs. They are always looking out for fun, to make a sharp remark or see the ridiculous, to play some funny trick or quiz you with a look. And from woods for miles about the joyous shout breaks out, the ringing laugh echoes, and thousands of brilliant flames mount crackling mid the lower leaves and branches of the oak and chestnut trees, diffusing warmth and lightness, brightness, over the scene, and dispelling the damp breath of the twilight dews that begin to moisten the grass and topmost forest leaves. Then the rude pot or cup of coffee is boiled upon the glowing embers and stirred round with a slender twig. Now it is being settled and when cool enough proves a delightful and exhilarating beverage for the mess.

Home Thoughts, From Abroad

After the evening repast they lie around the blazing log and talk of their various campaigns, or perhaps speak of their loved ones at home, wonder how long it will be before they will greet them again, and then they may grow silent and gaze into the glowing embers of the fire, and picture to themselves the forms of early years, the shapes and scenes of by-gone days, build castles in the flames and sigh and long for the time when war's loud roar shall cease and peace again pervade their homes.

More Prayer Meetings

Perhaps this is the night for prayer meeting, for the parsons, taking advantage of this period of calm, are indefatigable in their efforts to draw the soldiers together to sing psalms and assist at prayer. Hundreds and thousands respond to their call and the woods resound for miles around with the unscientific but earnest music of the rough veterans of Lee's army. In doleful contrast to the more enlivening notes of the initiated, the chorus of the 'Mourners' may often be recognized; for conversions among the non-religious members of the army of Lee are of daily occurrence, and when they establish themselves upon the 'Mourners' ' Bench, it is evident to all how deep and loud is their repentance. There is something very solemn in these immense choruses of earnest voices, and there are, I am sure, hundreds of these honest soldiers truly sincere in believing that they are offering their most acceptable service to God.

Some of the parsons or chaplains are very zealous and persevering in assembling the soldiers to prayer; especially the chaplain of the eleventh Va. and the seventh. The latter is held in high esteem by all, whether members of religion or not; for, they say, in times of action, he is as bold as the bravest and is to be seen in the first and fiercest battles, consoling and assisting the wounded. 'Florence McCarthy' of Richmond, chaplain of the 7th inf., is also distinguished for his preaching and zeal among the soldiers. They say he told his congregation the other day that when they heard the doors and windows of the church slamming while the minister of God was preaching, they might be sure that the devil was at work trying to hinder the faithful from listening to the divine word. Some might very naturally presume from this that his Satanic Majesty was most at large during the blustering month of March than at any other time in the year.

Some Distractions from Prayer

Our regiment at night, however, as I have said, instead of *reviving* themselves with prayer meetings are serenaded by Bill Dean's troupe who make the woods in our immediate vicinity reecho with all the old negro songs and glees that have been composed many years back. Another nightly occupation is to rob bee hives; and not infrequently when the choruses of hymns is ascending, parties return from a thieving expedition with hats filled with honey comb.

Lee Reorganizes

And now the various regiments are filling up again. The convalescent, sick, and wounded are returning, and conscripts are being received by the regiments. We receive between twenty five and thirty and have now as many men in our *company* as we had in the *Regiment* at Sharpsburg. Drills also begin to be of daily occurrence, the first in fact that we have been subjected to since the army left Manassas last Spring.

We are to be in two corps, Genl. Longstreet commands one and Stonewall, the immortal Jackson, the other. Longstreet's corps shall consist of, I think, the divisions of Generals McLaws, Pickett, Walker, and Hood. Jackson's corps will include A. P. Hill, Ewell, and Taliaferro who commands Jackson's old division. Gen. D. H. Hill, it is said, commands the reserves, whatever that may be, Genl. Pendleton the artillery, and the gay cavalier Stuart the much abused and much abusing cavalry (frequently termed the Calvary.)

Tedium of Drills

These daily drills, and regimental and brigade reviews and inspections, though very necessary and exceedingly useful, are felt by nearly all of us to be a *great bore*. For after 5 or 6 months of hard marching and fighting, to subside into the quiet and monotony and most tedious irksomeness of camp life goes very much against the private soldier. No sense of patriotism may influence him so far at this late season of the war, to undergo the trivial details of drills, etc., and I fear that an extra tour of guard duty has far more effect upon those who would be delinquent than all the patriotic sentiment that may be brought to bear. We all know, and some of our dear friends and comrades have known it, alas, too well, that 'dulce et decorum est pro patria mori', but the drilling and cleaning up the camp and keeping our muskets bright and clean,—ah, that is another thing! And then to be almost eaten alive by vermin that in myriad troops swarm through the camp and defy the boldest and the most hardened,—ah, these trials are not altogether so sweet as patriotism's first glow in the breast would have us imagine.

Camp Humor, Strictly Homespun

It is often amusing, although at times disgusting enough, to hear the oft repeated jests of our good humored and persevering comrades. Nothing happens in camp capable of being joked upon, but some camp wag must have his say. To strangers the jokes may appear ludicrous, as oftentimes they are in fact. But to us who have so often heard them, they have ceased to be funny unless some thing ridiculous accompanies the jest; as for instance if the one jested upon takes the matter seriously and shews temper or resents it in any manner. Then the general attention being called to the scene, the laugh becomes general and the sufferer departs in high dudgeon affording extravagant mirth when otherwise he would have only borne off the stale and ordinary joke.

Frequently the citizens have to pass by, and any kind of

linen shirt will bring down a cry upon them of 'come out of that *biled* (boiled) shirt; we know you're in thar; see the collar, etc.'; for the genuine soldier despises a 'biled' shirt, as being indicative of any easy position, unbelligerent duties, and a parade of gentility in these troublous war times. So no one, no matter how distinguished may be his appearance, is allowed to pass, wearing a linen shirt, unless he be strenuously and jocosely exhorted to divest himself of the objectionable article.

Perhaps the passing citizen's shirt collar is remarkably high and pointed. If so he is recommended to 'come from behind that collar; for it ain't no use a trying to conceal himself behind that flapper, for every body can distinguish his eyebrows'. Perhaps two men on the same animal go by. —'I say, you fellows, that's an imposition on that poor beast; give him double rations, for any animal doing double duty is entitled to double rations'.

Sometimes an officer or citizen strides along with boots nearly covering the entire leg. Immediately he is requested to come forth from *them boots*, 'taint no use hiding, for his *head is plainly visible!* If any one with long and exquisitely greased and twisted moustache rides by, he is told to 'take them mice out of his mouth; 'taint no use saying they ain't thar—see their tails a waggin' '. Again, some good old farmer with very large hat is urged to 'come from under that hat; he can't fool them—see his legs a dangling'. Another time a courier dashing by at *fool* speed is suddenly halted by the urgent cries of several breathless wags, and when he draws up to enquire the cause of his detention is provokingly told that his horse's caudal appendage is loose (or unscrewed), and if he is not very careful it will soon *drop out*. This is the most provoking joke of all and may be practiced only upon the uninitiated.

A Peculiarly (or Perhaps Doubtfully) Rich Joke

I heard a fellow the other day expostulating with a farmer. The farmer's mule, slowly moving along the road, had made several ineffectual efforts to scratch his hairy side with his hind hoof. Every time he would raise his hind hoof for this purpose and kick his itching side or belly, it had the exact appearance of trying to put his foot in the stirrup. Upon which an officious wag ran out from the wood and insisted upon the farmer getting down and *permitting the mule to get up* (on the farmer's back.) Such an extremely ridiculous idea never before occurred to me; and I believe it was greeted by the idlers of the camp as a particularly and peculiarly rich joke.

Boys Must Be Boys

At times there is a tremendous sudden wild and continued shouting, the whole bivouack is in confusion and wild commotion. Finally the cause is known, and a poor old hare (*old har*), frightened to death, or captured by the endless bands of pursuers, is dangled through the camp by his hind legs in the hands of his capturers [sic].

When the Generals Pass By

Again there is a perfect rush to the road side. The woods for miles are lined with dusky-brown home spun, grey and Grenshaw goods, coarse slate-colored garments, in fact all varieties of uniforms, and every shape and form and apology of hats and shoes. The owners of these motly uniforms are curiously and eagerly scanning the dusty road. From camp to camp the word has passed like wild fire, and cheer succeeding cheer announces in the distance that some one important is to be seen.

It may be either Gen. Jackson or 'Uncle Robert', as the boys call Genl. Lee. If the latter, he is riding, perhaps, with a few aides, dressed in a neat grey uniform, mounted upon a gently moving charger. By the plain grey uniform you would simply recognize him as a general. His hair and beard turning grey; his mildly beaming face, large black eyes recognizing all around him; his mouth firmly but pleasingly set, and his whole figure expressing gentleness, dignity, and command. As he passes the admiring throngs they doff their warworn hats and greet his presence with reiterated shouts and most enthusiastic. He answers each burst with a placid smile and with a dignified but most courteous bend of his noble head.

Stonewall Evades the Compliments

Should the attraction of the excited soldiery prove to be Stonewall Jackson, it may be that he passes by at full speed, nearly always in a canter and often covered with dust so thickly as almost to be unrecognizable. Cheer after cheer rings after him, which he acknowledges from time to time by doffing his forage cap or nodding kindly from right to left. But he is glad to be rid of the turmoil and cheering, and often puts spurs to his charger and is soon hidden in clouds of dust.

'Tantie' Returns From a Sad Mission

Thus day by day goes by wearily enough at times, but yet enlivened frequently by such excitement as I have just spoken of. Tantie Jones, my messmate, and Serjeant-Major of the Regt., has just returned to us. He accompanied the gallant young Garland Overton to Shepardstown and remained with him until his death which happened a few days ago. Garland was on Gen. Pryor's staff and was mortally wounded at Sharpsburg. Tantie being a near relation waited on the gallant officer until his death.

The Sharpsburgers Pay High for Their Fun

Tantie says that the people in Shepardstown, who are true Virginians, told him that they suffered the greatest persecution from the townsmen of Sharpsburg, not only by being continually spied, reported, and lied upon; but whenever the Sharpsburgers wished for a little extra amusement, they would bring down to the river bank a little cannon and shell the opposite and unoffending village of Shepardstown. Of course the latter dared not retaliate in any way, lest their town might be burned by the Yankees. When I heard this I could not help rejoicing to think of the terrific shelling administered to the worthy town of Sharpsburg upon the 16th and 17th ult., and the best of that fearful joke was that every shell dealing destruction throughout the devoted place came from their Yankee friends.

The Perils of Guard Duty

Nothing new transpires and we are beginning to feel very dull.[3] This evening I am detailed for guard duty which duty comes round very often while there are so few in the brigade and division to perform it. We are usually detailed for twenty four hours and during this time are separated from our command to be transferred to some other scene of action. This evening our rendezvous or guardhouse is at the foot of the hill on which is our bivouack, close by a dead hollow tree some seven or eight feet in height. Near this tree we make a crackling, roaring fire, and prepare to pass the night as comfortably as our guard duties may permit.

After pleasantly chatting by the blazing logs we wrap us in our blankets and all fall asleep.[4] The night is very cold

[3] There is a gap in Dooley's journal from late September until the end of the third week in October. He here picks up the story on October 18.

[4] We reluctantly conclude that Dooley's detachment were taking their guard duties very lightly.

and after midnight a high wind rises and sweeps boisterously over the fields. It blows with great force the sparks of our glowing fire into the hollow portions of the old apple tree and in a few moments the whole trunk is on fire top to bottom. Our blankets too are scorching and we wake just in time to save ourselves from quite a disastrous accident; for the cartridge boxes hung round the trunk and in the hollow were singeing under the application of the fierce flames and in a few seconds must have exploded all around our sleepy heads. A portion of my belt and cartridge box was burned to a crisp. Others fared worse than I, and although we saved our cartridges and escaped without material injury to our persons, alas! the tree was wholly destroyed.

Lee's Care for Yankee Property

Our guard duty is principally to guard a farmhouse near by, the house of a 'Yanko-Virginian', or Yankee who is settled in these parts. He has asked for protection and a guard, and being a Union man it must be granted at the expense of *our* comfort. This is policy, but it sours our men very much to think of the brutal destruction of property by our enemy, who has desecrated our homes; and now we approach hostile settlements to be commanded to respect private rights and property of renegades, and to be even seriously incommoded ourselves to give a little more ease and assurance to shameless traitors! Ah, well, two wrongs never make a right, and perhaps after all the man who owns this house is not a renegade as our grumbling fellows say.

The house is an old fashioned stone house, and the orders are that none of our soldiers shall dip water from the stream flowing through the property. At least every five minutes I am obliged to admonish the water carriers of the camp that they must draw water either above or below this hallowed enclosure. They grumble no little at this, but know, rebels though they be, that *orders must be respected.*[5]

More Drill, Under Difficulties

Oct. 21. This afternoon we have a regimental drill and none of our field officers being with the Regt., the Senior Capt. undertakes to put through the manoeuvres. The field in which we are moving is covered with old stumps of trees, some of them two or three feet high. Such obstacles being continually in our way, our evolutions are more comic than graceful and regular; but notwithstanding that we are oftentimes *stumped*, and the commanding officer is once or twice *laid low*, yet altogether our drill may be looked upon as a decided success, especially being the first of the season and initiating a series of like important movements.

Old Reuben Gives Limited Service

Oct. 25.[6] Old 'Reuben' arrives in camp this evening bringing letters and articles to several members of the Regt. This old —— [the adjective is undecipherable] goes round to our friends in Richmond and after collecting all the needful articles and letters that they will entrust him with, sets out for the Regt.; but on the road always *happens* to be *robbed* of about one half of his goods; when he arrives in camp he is *so glad to see everybody* (and in fact we are glad enough to see him), but his losses are terrible, he can't account for them, and to hear his moans and see his woe begone face you might think he was the most miserable and unfortunate of Negroes. But we all understand him, and so

[5] There are, however, many passages in Dooley's diary which make us wonder just how fervent was the Confederate soldier's submission to authority.

[6] Note that Dooley will often skip several days at a time, confining his entries to incidents which he considers worth recording.

do they at home; but so that we get half of what is sent we are satisfied and willing to let the rest go. He brings me two letters full of home news and interest.

A Very Special Review

Oct. 27. Orders for a grand review. Longstreet's whole corps to be reviewed by Genls. Lee, Longstreet and Pickett, and, as rumour spreads around, by two *noble Lords* from *England*. I tell you, such a parade as this does not come every day for Lee's ragged veterans, so we are busy all the morning burnishing our arms and accoutrements and arranging ourselves as tidy as the circumstances of camp life permit.

About two o'clock in the afternoon our brigades assemble for the review and direct their steps towards a field nearly a half mile distant. Here the whole corps soon arrives, some twenty thousand in number, and are scattered here and there over the field awaiting the preparations for the parade. The field is about a mile long and nearly half a mile wide, poles are erected in several places to direct the course of the moving columns, couriers and aides dash around the space in special haste, and after an hour and a half delay, the drums beat the roll and we all *fall in*.

The generals take their position on the left side of the field, and we begin our march, determined to look as well as possible before our leaders and the *foreigners*. Our Brigade occupies a central position in column, and as we pass these noble reviewers I am sure all of us looked our best, bore our arms with all the precision of which we knew, and wondered if the English Lords didn't admire us. In returning to Camp someone suggested that it would be mortifying and a sad joke if the Englishmen whom we had been trying to please so much were only Yankee spies; and I must confess I had myself some doubt about their genuine nobility.

Chapter Five

FREDERICKSBURG

OCT. 31. Still upon our old camping grounds and still under arms and ready for a move. These delays are really far worse than the march.

McClellan has crossed the Potomac and is moving cautiously in a southerly direction and we are waiting perhaps until his route becomes definitely known.[1] Towards noon we are on our way towards Winchester, which glorious little town we reach after an hour's march. We must pass through the town in good order. Therefore the ranks are formed and dressed, the drums are rattling, and whatever bands we have begin to do their best, while we march down the main street.

Winchester Turns Out to Cheer

Such an enthusiastic reception we never rec'd. before. The streets and windows are thronged with men, women and children almost frantic with delight to see their ragged grey rebels go by. Their deafening cheers, their excited gestures, their eager faces, all that we saw convinced us beyond all doubt that they were truly in earnest, and although we were leaving them to become again the helpless

[1] McClellan's army crossed the Potomac on Oct. 26. Lee, not knowing whether his opponent was heading for the Shenandoah valley or southward on the east side of the mountains, split his forces into two groups in order to head off the Federal commander in whatever direction the latter might move. Jackson was ordered to draw back to a point near Winchester, and Longstreet was directed to move over the Blue Ridge into Culpeper County. Dooley's description (immediately following) deals with this latter operation.

prey of an unfeeling and brutal foe, yet the very sight of our scarred and war torn veterans so aroused their old Virginian spirit that all thought of self and their own loss seemed to be forgotten or merged in the great idea of our glory and the benefit of the whole country. All praise and honour to noble Winchester, unfalteringly true to Old Dominion's flag, which though overwhelmed and trampled and outraged beneath the heel of low and contemptible tyrants, rose up manfully, victoriously again and again to the aid and encouragement of our struggling arms.

From Winchester we emerged upon the open turnpike leading directly South, and turning to our left before dark we have crossed the ——[undecipherable] creek, not without wetting our feet however, for the rail bridge by which we cross gives way in many places and our feet are as wet as though we had been crossing a river.

Home Thoughts Come at Night

By night fall we are again in bivouack making good fires, for the night is cold and our feet must be dried before we sleep.[2] Then thousands of fires gleam out from woods and even hill side, along the roads and deep within the forest glen, and sounds of mirth and song and jest rudely burst upon the wonted stillness of the solitude until the weary soldiers stretch their limbs before the burning embers and dream of the 'pleasant fields traversed so oft'.

Longstreet Falls Back Slowly Towards Fredericksburg

Nov. 1. We are on the road bright and early this morning approaching the Luray Valley. The song and jest go round from mouth to mouth and the cool fresh air of hill

[2] The ravages caused by the prolonged wearing of wet footgear has been made painfully evident to our armies in the war today.

top and woodland gives new vigor to our limbs and lightness to our hearts.

And now we are nearing the Shenandoah, leaving Strasburg on our right. (Strasburg, famous for the precipitate retreat of Banks' army last spring when Jackson was trying to catch him; and in fact he did overtake his discomfited rear at Middletown, and pretty work did his artillery make among the panic stricken masses that thronged the turnpike. He pursued them again from Winchester until they rested panting upon the borders of the Potomac; and Abraham trembling in the white house called for a new army to keep back that terrible Jackson.)

Ravaged Virginia

As we pass through the Shenandoah valley I think how in the days of peace and prosperity every hamlet and stream, every vale and mountain, hilltop and mead, of our own loved Virginia, was teeming and resplendent with fertility, loveliness and grandeur. But now alas! How is it now? From Staunton to the Potomac scarce a farmyard that is not stained with human blood, scarce a stream but has been tinged by the life current of some of Virginia's bravest; scarce a field unpolluted by the enemy's touch, scarce a hill top unploughed by the iron missiles of death. The fences are burned, the meadows trampled down, the cattle all gone and the harvests unharvested; proud homesteads in ruins, the masters on the war trail and the old couple and daughters sit mournful and comfortless around expiring embers. Oh war, war! Cruel, bloody war! Little did they know who wished for this! Oh, may they never know peace in this life who have forced this diabolical alternative upon our noble land.

Condition of the Army

The weather is now getting quite wintry and we must defend ourselves against its vigors as best we can. The army is in a wretched condition as regards tents, blankets, shoes and warm clothing. Many of the men are either barefoot or their feet are protected by such scant portions of leather that they are not unfrequently [sic] exposed to the dangers of being frost bitten. Our rations are of beef and bread and are generally enough, *especially* if we may get some extras now and then from home or the sutler's tent.

A Blanket Solution

We[8] have but four blankets between us, so we must manage economically. The way we adopt is for all three to sleep together, lying on one blanket and covering with the other three. This arrangement is all very well with respect to the length of the blankets, but the width is another matter. Provided we all lie in the same position the blankets cover us snugly enough; but if one takes a different position from the other two, the blankets fail to accommodate all. Seeing the dilemma in which we are placed we make the following agreement: We shall all go to sleep in the same position and if during the night one awakes and wishes to turn over, he must not do so without giving previous warning, when, all being ready, the movement shall be effected. So now when some one of us awakes during the night and wishes for a 'change of base', he wakes up the others and announces his purpose. Thereupon all being thoroughly awake the man in the middle gives the com-

[8] That is, Dooley and his two messmates 'Tantie' Jones and Willie Mitchel. The latter was only 17 years old and had just joined the regiment. He will be killed at Gettysburg.

mand 'right' or 'left turn', and the movement is made promptly and without disorder.

We often laugh at ourselves for this arrangement, but it is the most comfortable way we can think of; and besides we have come to the conclusion that the most objectionable part of it has its advantages also. For, if we are obliged to undergo the unpleasantness of being aroused at midnight for the convenience of one of our number, we also enjoy our night's rest even more by interrupting it, than if we took it all at one snooze. Ned, our servant, lies out side the shelter, and wrapped in his blanket rolls close to the fire, with his feet in the ashes and often missing but by little of burning his toes.

Religion in the First Virginia Volunteers

Our chaplain leaves us at this camping ground, desirous to look out for a situation more congenial to his tastes and habits. And as the Methodist Conference meets in a few weeks he has obtained leave of absence to attend the meeting, where he expects to enter upon a *holier* and more profitable sphere of duties than he has found life in camp, especially among the members of the 1st Va. Inf. to afford him.

In fact, the members of our Regt. are the most indifferent set of fellows, as to prayer meetings, I ever saw. A great many of them read their Bibles quite piously, particularly upon the eve of a battle, and on Sunday they don't object to singing hymns or hearing an eloquent exhortation. But they won't go a hundred yards to indulge in a prayer meeting. The difference between them and the other Regts. around us is no doubt partly attributable to our boys being for the most part young and *all* from the City, and in nearly all the other Regiments there is a much larger portion of country-raised men. Besides, to the best of my knowledge our parson has never made a serious effort to make a convert or establish a prayer meeting in the Regiment, and probably it was just as well to save himself the trouble. At any rate we are a *very* irreligious body of young men, and Bill Dean's opera troupe is very popular among us from seven till 9 o'clock every night.

Punishments

I would like to tell you how breakers of discipline are treated. All prisoners of the Regt. are consigned to the guard house and if they prove refractory are liable to be *bucked* or gagged. Some times refractory members of companies are sent to the guard house under condemnation either to be bucked or gagged or perhaps to wear a barrel-shirt.

'Bucking' is making the culprit sit in a doubled up posture, clasping his knees with his hands, and whilst his knees almost touch his chin a long stick is inserted between his arms and underneath his knee joints. 'Gagging' is more severe, and is performed by placing a bayonet in the culprit's mouth and fixing it there by tying behind the head strings or cord attached to either end of the implement of torture. Frequently however a stick is used in place of the bayonet on account of the severity of the former instrument. Should the condemned resist or become very insolent, he is shown no mercy until he evinces some marks of repentance and future subordination. Usually neither of these two punishments lasts more than from an hour to two hours.

The barrel shirt punishment is generally inflicted upon such as have been guilty of some petty or shameful misdemeanors and have been sentenced by a court martial to this ignominious and ludicrous mode of expiation. The barrel shirt is simply a flour barrel minus both head and bottom, with two holes made in the staves. The culprit is clothed with this staving garment, thrusts his arms through the holes, gets his chin over the rim, and has to walk up and down a given space under guard for as many hours during the day as are appointed by his sentence. He finds it quite embarrassing and his legs are at a loss how to proceed. I have never seen any one hung up by the thumbs, which punishment, they say, is very frequent in the Yankee army. I have seen however what may be thought a novel punishment for an offense by no means unusual. Some of the men being caught in the act of straggling from their regiments were brought back and made to march in a circle, like horses working a threshing machine, at the same time having billets of wood tied to their ankles in order to impede their progress. But this novelty I have seen but once.

Train Whistles and Thoughts of Home

As we march on towards Culpepper[4] C. H. a train of cars passes by within a few hundred yards, and the whistle awaking a thousand echoes in the neighboring woods, sounds more joyfully in my ears than anything I can remember now. What scenes of blood and carnage, what sounds of war had filled my eyes and ears since last I heard the whistling of the peaceful locomotive! I feel revivified, electrified from head to foot, and seem to be already within a few miles of my home in Richmond-town. But this is a *deception*, for as the cars roll by and I watch them disappear in the direction of Culpepper I find myself trudging along the frightful roads more than a hundred miles from that beloved spot so attractive to friend and foe. But perhaps

[4] Here and subsequently Dooley will insist on putting an extra 'p' in Culpeper.

we are going there, for our road is in that direction; at least so far it has been almost directly South.

Extra Aids on the March

We are trying to raise sufficient funds among the rear guard to buy a quart of apple brandy. This beverage is not very abundant in the country, but one of the guard knows where he can obtain a quart of it if he has only sixteen dollars. For the dealer in this precious drink will not sell less than a quart, nor a quart for less than sixteen dollars. Alas! for the poverty of the guard. He cannot raise sixteen dollars in Confederate Scrip.

Incident of the Frisky Adjutant

Much fun had the boys today in my absence.[5] They told me that our gallant adjutant had quite distinguished himself and his equestrian fame shall be henceforth indubitable. After leaving Culpepper he became so dashing that he nearly dashed a portion of the Regiment to pieces. Spurring on his fiery steed he would gallop frantically thru the whole length of the Regt., several being knocked down who were not nimble enough to avoid the furious charge. Then he would scamper across the field at a mad pace, his charger refusing no fence or wall that came in the way. He is a splendid rider and his horse took the fences like the best trained hunter; and it was a beautiful sight to gaze after him plunging over the surrounding country. But now and then he would return to the Regt. and charge through our friends; and this proved not so pleasant. This continued for several hours and the last time the gallant adjutant incommoded our company, our Capt. drew a pistol on him and told him in a voice not to be misunderstood that if he came

[5] There is obviously a connection between this paragraph and the one immediately preceding.

near his company again, he would shoot him. After this abrupt decision the adjutant disappeared in the distance and only returned, sobered a little, before the Regt. went into night quarters.

The Regiment Asks for More

After marching all day[6] we find ourselves towards evening in need of rations and amuse ourselves by shouting this aloud as we proceed along the road. Soon after an announcement semi-official is made informing us that our wants shall be attended to; and by and by, Gen. Kemper and his staff together with Commissary Major Green, Serjeant Jennings, etc. ride by at full speed; which movement we, misinterpreting as a notification of speedy bivouack and fresh rations, cheer most lustily again and again. Gen. Kemper politely raises his hat as often as our acclamations are reiterated, and we are soon moving into night quarters anticipating a substantial meal of bread and coffee.

Strategic Situation, Late November 1862

And now our move towards Fredericksburg is being discussed; Madam Rumour saith that the successor of McClellan—Burnside—has entertained a tremendous notion in his head and after treating it with due consideration has determined to put it in execution: viz., instead of trying to overcome us by main force he will move over to Fredericksburg, take possession of that splendid position and march to Richmond by that route. But Gen. Stuart has his eyes wide open and so has Uncle Robert. So that the first indi-

[6] It was now sometime between November 15–17. Burnside was marching against Fredericksburg (as a stepping-stone to Richmond). Longstreet's corps was heading for Fredericksburg to checkmate the Union general there. At this point in his journal Dooley is sparing of his dates, to the embarrassment of the editor.

cation of a move in that direction causes Gen. Robert to reinforce the garrison on the hills at Fredericksburg, and to follow up with the whole corps of Longstreet, the rearguard of which are we.

Lee Talks Back

The boys say that the other day when the Yankees sent over word for the surrender of the town [Fredericksburg] that they were astounded to receive an answer from Uncle Robert himself bidding them to 'come and take it'. Whether our great leader was there or not, it is evident that the Yankees found our friends ready for them and upon receiving the intimation that if they wished to take possession of the town it would be necessary to cross the Rappahannock, came to the conclusion that not having expected so much opposition to their plans, they would wait a few days and see if more favorable terms might not be obtained. At any rate the boys say that everything is safe under lock and key, Gen. Lee being in possession of both. Hence we have been jogging along at a moderate pace, making our fifteen or sixteen miles a day, and not even knowing where we are going.

Dooley Foregoes a Good Show

Nov. 21.[7] Today we continue upon the pike and I feel very stiff and weary, so much so that being called to the side of the road to witness a cavalry review, I could not muster sufficient energy to drag myself thither. The review was of a division or two of Stuart's cavalry, in an adjoining field; but it would be necessary for me to mount a bank three or four feet above the road to get a good view; the

[7] Here Dooley has apparently made a slip in his chronology. By the 21st, Longstreet had already reached his position at Fredericksburg. However, it is possible that his *rear guard* (where Dooley is) could have been still en route to Fredericksburg as late as the 21st.

exertion is too much for my present condition of weariness, and I trudge on wishing for the end, but afterwards deploring my want of enterprise in not taking a look at the cavalry exercises; for the boys spoke so much about them that I became envious. In fact, most of those who saw the review declare they have never witnessed so large a body of horse together; and as for me I have never seen more than a Regiment of Cavalry together, so much aloof are the infantry of our Corps and the Cavalry kept.

We soon strike into the —— [?] and after considerable delay bivouack on the low thickets back of the hills overhanging Fredericksburg and close to a small stream delighting in the name of 'Deep Run'. Here we prepare to rest a few days awaiting the determination of our Yankee opponents whom, deadly enemies though they be, we do not wish to refuse a warm Virginian welcome should they decide to cross the Rappahannock. . .[8]

One night we[9] receive a little sugar and coffee and about a quart of whiskey from home. The night is very cold and so we agree to make whiskey punch. So we make a fire and put on the water, determining to have the punch *schreeching* hot. But as we formed the resolution late, it was long after taps before we got everything ready. But all things being concocted, we enjoyed a cozy little time, I assure you, by our glowing camp fire, reflecting how cold it was without us and how snug within. And as we had much more than we wanted or was good for us we took the remainder to George Norton, our Capt., and Pete Kunningham (Lieut.),

[8] Longstreet's Division (Dooley accompanying) took up its position, November 19, on the hills behind Fredericksburg, and, firmly entrenched, awaited the Federal attack. On the same day Burnside had arrived at Falmouth, opposite Fredericksburg. John Dooley seems to have neglected his journal somewhat from this time until the opening of the battle on December 13.

[9] That is, Dooley, Tantie Jones, and Willie Mitchel.

and Lieut. Reeves, and awakened them by placing the hot punch beside their faces. They were startled, but enjoyed the joke.

Preliminaries to Fredericksburg

*We had not been here many days before the Yankees began crossing the river, which we were unable to prevent owing to the splendid position their batteries occupied on the hills opposite, which protected their passage. Gen. Lee was prepared for them however, and we were out on picket for a week, the weather being intensely cold.

Dooley's Regiment Held in Reserve During the Battle

At length on the morning of the 13th of December they had all crossed and we joined battle on the right about 11 or 12 o'clock in the day.[10] Finally the action became general along our whole line, and about 3 P.M. we were ordered to take position on the extreme left.[11] After double quicking for several miles we thought we had gained our halting place; but we were shifted here and there during the evening so as to be in supporting distance of other divisions should they need our assistance.[12]

[10] This 'we' does not apply to Kemper's brigade, which, throughout the entire action, was held in reserve. Burnside opened the battle with an attack on the Confederate right flank. This end of the Confederate line was driven back dangerously far, and was finally saved from complete collapse only by Early's timely counter-attack.

[11] "Burnside had shifted his battle to Longstreet's front in one of the most ghastly and dramatic assaults of American war." (Freeman, *op. cit.*, II, 358.)

[12] "After 2 o'clock, as the attack on Jackson on the Confederate right was collapsing, he [Longstreet] decided that he could safely reduce force on his right to strengthen his center. He sent therefore to Pickett for two Brigades. Kemper's he put in reserve for Ransom. . ." (Freeman, *op. cit.*, II, 365.) Dooley's reference to Kemper's brigade being 'shifted here and there, etc.' suggests aptly a very important fact about this battle, viz., Longstreet's highly intelligent handling of his units so as to plug up the weak spots in the Confederate line as soon as they appeared.

With the moans and cries of the dying enemy in our ears, we (Co. D) set about providing a defense against the enemy's sharp shooters, so that we too may not be groaning and dying when the morrow's night arrives. We set about the work of making a stone wall.

While we worked at this fence the most dismal moans and groans and the most piteous cries seem to arise on all sides of us. The nearest fallen of the Yankees were not over thirty-five yds. from us, and we could distinctly hear their cries for help, their curses, groans and prayers, all of them mingling in mournful discord; and the ambulances of the Yankees moved so close to us that we thought sometimes they were coming among us. Several parties did ride in among us during the night, and were very much surprised to learn from us how they had done it. We however could not let such opportunities slip by without extending to them our hospitality altho' our bitterest enemies, and we got them to stay with us all night and how much longer I don't know.*

Fredericksburg Anti-climax

14th December.[13] As the mist began partially to clear away, a warning came down the lines that the Yanks were advancing, and the whole brigade discharged their pieces almost simultaneously at what we supposed to be the Yankees. However, as the volley attracted no notice from the Yankees and as they didn't seem to advance very fast, we cooled down a little and looking more steadfastly at the

[13] The battle had ended in a bloody repulse for the Federals, who thereupon decided to postpone their drive on Richmond until the Spring.

object supposed to be a line of blue coats, we concluded it must be a fence, which, when the mists cleared away, it turned out to be. . .[14]

[14] After Fredericksburg, Longstreet's corps first settled into winter quarters near Petersburg; then, after several shifts of location, moved into the Suffolk-Blackwater area, with the purpose of establishing a base for foraging expeditions into North Carolina. For the next few months John Dooley will have no battles to describe. The staple of his journal until early May 1863 will be the incidents of camp life,—some of them routine and some decidedly colorful. He leaves large gaps in the record, but gives us many a *genre* picture of Lee's army at comparative rest during that six-months' lull before the great storm of Gettysburg.

Chapter Six

PAUSE BEFORE GETTYSBURG

DEC. 25. Today we move camp towards Petersburg, and it being Christmas day a great many of the Regt. receive from home boxes containing whiskey and other good things wherewith to enjoy ourselves and celebrate the day. Pa sends me a jug of whiskey and we all get quite *agreeable* at night.

28th of Dec. Moved camp again today and encamp within 5 miles of Guiney's Station, very near the railroad to Richmond. Willie, Tantie and I, with Ned assisting, rear a log cabin for ourselves and then plaster it over with mud. . .

Surcease From War

During the winter we have several visits from our folks in Richmond, who supply us with good things in general and whiskey in particular to boot. Mr. and Mrs. Kunningham[1] give the whole Regt. a dinner, and many happy nights did we pass, singing and carousing in our huts or in Capt. Norton's tent. . .[2]

[1] Keiningham.

[2] During the first two months of 1863 Dooley's regiment was not always stationary. In mid-February it was sent to the line of works above Fredericksburg in order to strengthen the defences near the Rappahannock. It then returned to Richmond, camped later at Manchester, and moved again to Chester Station, where it remained until March 1st. From March 1st until March 15th it was in camp near Prince George Court House; on the 15th it was ordered to Fort Powhatan. On April 11th it was in camp on the Blackwater; it arrived near Suffolk on April 13th, and remained there until May 3rd.

This evening[3] (March 9, 1863) our Brigade is ordered out to witness a horrible sight.[4] One of the 24th Va. Infantry being tried by court martial for cowardice at the battle of Sharpsburg is condemned to be whipped publicly and then dishonorably dismissed from the service. The brigade is to be present at this degrading punishment.

We are all drawn up in line and the poor man is tied to a pole about fifty yards in front of us. His hands are stretched above his head and his shirt stripped to the waist. The executioner then steps forward and with several heavy switches, the executioner being likewise a criminal who is to earn his release from punishment by inflicting this disgrace on his fellow man.

A Sad Spectacle

The word being given, the executioner began his disgusting work, the wretched man wincing and his flesh shrinking neath every blow which one after another were delivered in quick succession until 39 were rec'd. by the culprit. In truth it is a horrid sight, and the executioner was so overcome by his feelings that as soon as his work was done his eyes filled with tears and he wept—he wept! This horrible event transpired without the loss of blood to any one, and the wretched creature (or happy individual, had he truly a craven heart) pockets his dishonorable discharge and leaves for parts unknown.

10th March. Today is the most wet and disagreeable of days and we are compelled to seek shelter wherever we can. A good many of us intruding ourselves into the Adjutant's tent resolve to have a song. And as there is one among us who sings an excellent song and sings it well, too, we en-

[3] Since late December there has been a long silence in the journal. Dooley here resumes his day-by-day account.

[4] They are now in camp near Prince George Court House.

gage all our arts of persuasion in inducing him to delight our senses by pouring forth the melodious notes of 'Bowed down.' Mr. Archibald Goven was a singularly constituted as well as peculiarly gifted young gentleman. His early days had been passed in Darby town, a village several miles from Richmond, through which although many persons have passed, and in which although many individuals have lived, still notwithstanding all these facts nevertheless no one has ever yet had any definite idea of its precise situation. Even Mr. Archibald Darby Goven, more facetiously and familiarly known as simple 'Darby,' did not know exactly where the place of his nativity was, but had a vague notion that it was not very far from Bottomses' Bridge in White Oak Swamp. Darby's earliest recollections as he himself told us were anything but pleasant. He had a cruel mother and a father probably not more kind. His parents' custom was to strip him of his clothing and fasten him to the Bed post and then beat him cruelly. When Darby grew older he was bound out to the owner of some charcoal kilns and in this employment, from intense application and the injurious effects of the gas his eyesight was materially injured. Later in life Darby was promoted to the summit of a charcoal cart and made the streets of Richmond resonant with his shrill yet melodious cries of 'charcoal, char-coal, cha-coal, *char-coal* ! ! Indeed even now upon being importuned by a large audience he makes the forest ring with these sweet notes, which are always received with unbounded applause, driving away all sadness from the heart and infusing new life into soul and body. But not to digress too far: Darby being asked to *chaunt* 'Bowed down' (such being our fondness for this song that Darby had delighted our ears with it per special request every evening for the past 6 months), owing to his extreme modesty excused himself from singing by remarking on the dampness of the weather and the numerous company assembled. Many objections did he bring forward, all of which were over ruled by his eager crowd of admirers; and he finally agreed to sing upon condition only that we should deny ourselves the pleasure of the song for the next three succeeding evenings. Here upon Darby commences in his *clear and charcolean* voice, his *nasal organs* joining in and the crowd doing the same when the chorus is reached. Thus runs the Song or the words thereof; 'tis a moral song and singularly characteristic of the simplicity of the manners and customs of the people among whom it was composed.

Camp near Petersburg. Song as sung fifteen times with immense applause in two hours, by Mr. Archibald D. Goven, upon 10th of March 1863, Adjutant's tent 1st Regt. Va. Vols:—

Song — slow, con expressione.

There was an old woman in yonder's countrie
Bow down! Bow down! (chorus)
There was an old woman in yonder's countrie
The bow is bent for me (higher)
There was an old woman in yonder's countrie (still higher)
She had daughters one—two—three!
(chorus forte) That I'll be true, true to my love,
My love is so true to me!

2nd Verse

The oldest bought the youngest a beaver,
Bow down! Bow down!
The oldest bought the youngest a beaver,
The bow is bent for me!

The oldest bought the youngest a beaver,
And she thought hard of that!
That I'll be true, true to my love,
My love is so true to me!

[5][*Note:* These verses have never been explained. The beaver however purchased by the oldest at which offense appears to have been taken is supposed by many to be a fashionable hat worn at that period among the well-to-do country folk.]

3rd Verse

Oh Sister, oh Sister, let's take a walk,
Bow, etc.
Oh Sister, oh Sister, let's take a walk,
The bow is bent for me!
Oh Sister, oh Sister, let's take a walk
To see their ships go sailing off—
That I'll be true, true to my love,
My love is so true to me!

[*Note:* The time of their perambulations appears to have been after nightfall; and, if the writer [i.e. Dooley] might be allowed a suggestion, one of the ships contained the lover of the maidens who are both attracted by the same person.]

4th Verse

As they were walking all on the se brim,
Bow down, etc.
As they were walking, etc.
The bow is bent, etc.
As they were walking all on the se brim
The oldest pushed the youngest one in—
That I'll be true, true to my love,
My love is so true to me.

[*Note:* The above stanza needs but little explanation. The two sisters appear to have been discussing the choice of the One to whom both were pledged, and the oldest in a fit of jealousy pushed her young sister into the sea whence the sequel saith she could not be rescued.]

[5] This and the subsequent bracketed notes are Dooley's.

5th Verse

The Sister did scream and the water did shake,
    Bow down, etc.
The Sister did scream and the water did shake,
    The bow is bent, etc.
The Sister did, etc.,
Saying far-you-well, Sister, I'll meet you at last,
        That I'll be true, true to my love,
        My love is so true to me.

[*Note:* The above stanza describes the agony of the drowning girl, the perturbation of the waters and the last words of the victim.]

6th Verse

'Oh Sister, oh Sister, oh give me your hand,
    Bow down, etc.,
'Oh Sister, oh Sister, oh give me your hand,
    The bow is bent, etc.
And you shall have my house and land,
        That I'll be true, true to my love,
        My love is so true to me.

[*Note:* Here new energy seems to possess the drowning victim and she pleads for life; she is willing to give all her possessions for her life.]

7th Verse

'I neither will give you my hand nor my glove,
    Bow down, etc.,
'I neither will give you my hand nor my glove,
    The bow is bent, etc.
'I neither will give you my hand nor my glove,
But I will marry your true love,
        That I'll be true, true to my love,
        My love is so true to me.

[*Note:* The Sister refuses all aid, even her glove, and persists in the ruin of her sister—to marry as she now avows her true love.]

8th Verse

They walked and talked until about eleven,
Bow down, etc.,
They walked, etc.,
The bow is bent, etc.
They walked and talked until about eleven,
Saying far-you-well, Sister, I'll meet you in heaven,
That I'll be true, true to my love,
My love is so true to me.

[*Note:* Much difficulty arises here and it is very likely that the above stanza has a different place in the original manuscript. But I give it the place assigned it by 'Darby,' not daring to alter anything that I heard from his lips.]

9th Verse

The Fisherman came with his fishing hook,
Bow down, etc.,
The Fisherman came, etc.,
The bow is bent, etc.
The Fisherman came with his fishing hook
But she was then just drownded in the brook,
That I'll be true, true to my love,
My love is so true to me.[6]

[*Note:* This fine alley [sic] is very sad. A Fisherman arrives upon the Spot but just too late to be of any service. He has an enormous fishing hook but upon raising the body it is found that life is wholly extinct. Tragic end of too devoted love! The word brook is here used instead of sea by way of poetic license and especially as it rhymes with hook.]

A Small Misstep and an Opportune Election

April 10. Today I am on extra tour of Guard duty for absence from roll call when at Jack Keily's the other night.[7]

[6] This is a corruption of the old Scottish ballad called variously "Binnorie" and "The Twa Sisters." For two divergent renderings *cf.: The Oxford Book of Ballads*, (ed. A. Quiller-Couch), Oxford, 1910, 104–106, and *Bibliotheca Curiosa: a Ballad Book*, (ed. E. Goldsmid), Edinburgh, privately printed, 1891, part 1, pp. 31–34.

[7] Keily was Quartermaster of the Post and an old friend of Dooley's.

But about 9 A.M. I am relieved by Company C electing me a Lieut. in their Company.

And here I will take occasion to explain the Cause of my election. In the first place, Capt. H., Co. C, had signified to the Col. his desire of having me as one of his Lieuts. It being decided by some authority that the Col. or Brigadier could not appoint a first Lieut., an election was held. A large majority of the members of Co. C were conscripts, new men in the Regt.; the old members were only 5 or 6. The new members, greatly in the majority, desired to elect one of their own number; and the old members, together with the Capt. and Col. of the Regt., were some what *predisposed* in my favor.

Everything Above Board (for the Most Part!)

It has been maliciously said that the new men or conscripts were *bullied into electing me* by threats from the minority. But *that*, I was told, was not the Case, and the only intimidation held out to them was by our Col. presiding over the election, who told the Company in case any *raw recruit was elected* that he would instantly have him *examined before the board.*[8] The party opposed to my election, thinking that their candidate could not stand the test of an examination, abandoned him and voted for Lieut. Kehoe of Company J. This vote was pretty equally divided, and on a second ballot *I was told* that I was elected.

If there was any unfairness in the election I do not know of it, and would rather have remained all my life in the ranks than to have permitted myself to be elected by means the least unfair. I say this much because I thought I observed one or two times the *slightest insinuation* in the world concerning my election, even from those who were my

[8] It was not precisely pressure that was being brought to bear on the conscripts, but they were certainly receiving some mild suggestions!

friends and who seemed to have been under a false impression.

Two or three days before the election I was promised the whole 'conscript' vote (by one of the leading recruits) if I would only promise if elected to serve their interests. I told the person who waited on me that I should give no promise whatever, that I had never asked anyone's vote nor did I intend to do so. I had not even asked any one to propose me for a candidate. He said the new members would all vote against me unless I made this promise, and I responded 'Allright' (or its equivalent), so that today when my election was announced, I was a little surprised and asked an explanation from the Capt. of the change in the men's votes. His explanation was that given above. . .[9]

May 3. We begin marching towards Franklin after dark,

[9] From mid-April to the beginning of May, Longstreet encamped in the Suffolk-Blackwater area for the following reason: the army of Northern Virginia was desperately in need of food supplies, and Longstreet's function was to collect as much of such supplies as possible from the less ravaged sections of North Carolina, and to forward the food to Lee who, with the major portion of the Army, was on the line of the Rappahannock above Richmond. After Hooker's raid on Port Royal, April 23, Lee began to consider the advisability of summoning Longstreet up from Suffolk to reinforce the defensive lines on the Rappahannock. On April 29 Lee received word that Hooker had crossed that river just west of Fredericksburg. On that same day, the Confederate Commander-in-Chief ordered Longstreet to leave the Suffolk front and join the Army on the Rappahannock. After a delay of several days (for Longstreet presented to Lee an alternative plan of sending Hood and Pickett to the aid of Johnston in Tennessee) Longstreet is by May 3 on his march northward to join Lee. He will, however, be too late to help Lee in the crucial battle of Chancellorsville (May 2–6). Almost a month later Longstreet will still be south of Tappahannock.

John Dooley makes no mention of these strategical considerations. He picks up the story on May 3, when Longstreet's corps is on its way northward to join Lee. A few weeks later this march will merge with the complicated and momentous action of the Gettysburg campaign.

8 P.M. March steadily all night through swamps and water even up to our waists.

May 4th. Still marching, and every citizen we meet—'How far to the Quay?' we ask. 'About a mile and a half,' is the invariable answer, and for two hours we are advancing to the Quay (as we thought), and got no nearer than before.

A Brief Trip Home on Business

10th.[10] Obtain a permit to visit Richmond to collect some money due to our company by appropriation of the city Council, made some time ago. Find my folks at home seated at the dinner table.

As my permission to be in Richmond is unlimited in regard to time, or rather limited to such time as I may finish the business entrusted to my care, I have a pleasant little sojourn for four or five days at home.[11] Finally on the 15th inst. I obtain an interview with Mr. —— of the City Council who in a very bland and courteous manner gives me the amount due our company, and to my utter astonishment asks me to speak a word in his favor (to my men) at the approach of the next election. Well, thinks I, here's a go—farewell to delicacy of feeling when you want office.

John Dooley Overstays His Leave

Having accomplished the main object of my visit, I am now supposed to be ready to join again my regiment, and should, strictly considering the case, do so; but hearing from so many reliable sources that our brigade will *for certain* pass through Richmond tonight, I don't care about

[10] Note that this is four days after the battle of Chancellorsville. Dooley and his regiment have been nowhere near this action, although it would seem to be the nearly unanimous opinion of the experts that they should have been.

[11] Dooley is very reticent about details of this visit to home.

marching 7 miles to meet it, and then return immediately. So I determine to remain where I am, especially as I have an engagement with Capt. M. to go to the Theatre tonight. At supper my Father tells me that Col. Williams (my Col.) had been in the store during the evening and threatened to place me in arrest if I did not rejoin the regiment during the night. Notwithstanding this terrible menace I determine to brave every consequence and remain in town tonight.

An Unfortunate *Rencontre*

Unfortunately as we are leaving the theatre Col. Williams joins us at the door, and, after speaking with my brother and Capt. M. for a little while, returns to camp without deigning a word to me. However, I do not consider that he has a right to place me in arrest unless I am absent without permission for 24 hours, which I am not; for my permission extended to such time as I should obtain the money which I came to collect. And although I waited every day upon the city Council, I did not effect my purpose until 3 P.M. today, and consequently if I am present tomorrow morning with my Company, I shall not have been absent twenty four hours.

May 16th. This morning I am with my company before Sunrise and before the Colonel is awake. He looks at me very suspiciously and I begin to fear that his threat of arrest is about to be executed. But he spares me as yet, and our Division is formed outside of Manchester for its entry into this little town and Richmond. I have been equipped with sword and uniform at home and now am in command of my own and a portion of another's company.

Jackson's Death Has Taken the Heart out of Richmond

In Manchester people were more demonstrative than in Richmond, where, although the street corners are crowded with sympathizing friends, there is no noisy demonstration as upon a former occasion. It may be that the sad loss of our trust-inspiring general, whose funeral cortege has so lately moved through the streets we are so enlivening with our parade, has sobered the public mind, and their most engrossing thought may be, Who will fill great Stonewall Jackson's place, who indeed can ever replace our noble hero, so pure, so truly great? Oh, words fail when the soldier would utter Jackson's praises! But he shall live in history's pages and in the hearts of the pure and the brave, when the dastardly government against which he drew his unblemished sword, shall for centuries have lain in ruin and disgrace!

Dooley Under Arrest

Father walks by my side until we reach Brook Avenue and then bids me good bye.

We stop in the afternoon upon the Turnpike 13 miles from Richmond, and I am soon summoned before Col. W., who informs me that it is his painful duty to place me in arrest. I hand him my sword quite cooly, and return to my friends. Capt. H. who is in the city still will also be placed under arrest when he returns. I am not sorry for myself because I do not consider that I am much to blame; and I am now free to go any where in the vicinity of the camp that I choose, having none of the official burdens and many of the privileges. Our company is now without an officer.[12]

[12] It is interesting to recall the attitude assumed by Major John Dooley (John's father) in a similar case of A.W.O.L. The incident occurred while Major Dooley was in temporary command of the 1st. Virginia Infantry Regiment in February 1862: "On one occasion Sergeant Morris, of Company G, reported some of the men of his company as having gone to Richmond without leave. To which the Major replied: 'And have they? the bad fellows! Let me know when they come back, and I will punish them severely!' A few days after, the Sergeant reported that they had returned. 'Have they come back? the good fellows!' was the Major's remark, and that was about the last of that." (Loehr, *op. cit.*, 15.)

A Brief and Pleasant Imprisonment

May 17th. Capt. H. returns and is placed under arrest and Lieut. Kehoe of Co. J is placed in command of our Co. C until further notice.

May 21st. Move camp to Taylorsville. I have but little to do save lounge around camp and enjoy myself. Mr. Mitchel and my two Sisters pay us a visit and we spend the day very pleasantly in the adjoining woods.[13]

22nd. Considering the dearth of officers and that Kehoe is needed in his own company, the Col. releases me from arrest and restores me to the command of Co. C. Of this I am sorry, for I have been having a pleasant vacation while in arrest and hoped it would continue for some time.

Dooley as Drillmaster

I drill the Company and am appointed officer of the day for tomorrow. While here at Taylorsville we have daily evening battalion drills, of which I know nothing in the world. In vain do I take Harder's Tactics in hand and try to study out the manoeuvres. The weather is so oppressive that I invariably lay the book aside and trust to luck to hear what the Col. says and understand what he means. The worst of all is that I am always in charge of a company, although the newest and most ignorant officer in the Regt. I listen however very attentively to the commands as they are enunciated and with one or two blunders come forth from these hard trials with credit to myself and company. During these days I slip down to Richmond for a day or two and have an opportunity of going to confession.

[13] Longstreet, it would appear, is breaking no speed records in order to come up with Lee.

Chapter Seven

THE GETTYSBURG CAMPAIGN

JUNE 3rd. This morning we are marching towards Tappahannock. Resting upon the road side [i.e. as we rest by the road side] a courier rides by, and a little dog belonging to one of the soldiers flies at the horse's heels, all the while barking furiously. The courier, indignant at this unmannerly interruption, loses all patience, checks his horse's speed, and drawing his cavalry sword makes a gallant charge. The whole Division sets up deafening huzzas as they witness the act of bravery, and the unfortunate courier rides off completely crestfallen and the subject of numberless sarcasms from the laughing troops.

March Through Culpeper C.H.

June 15th. Resume our march, passing through Culpepper [sic] C.H. The heat is frightful, and the road in many places is strewn with the *sunstruck*. I stand the sun better than some of the stoutest of my men; and perceiving one of my poor fellows in great distress on account of his gun and accoutrements, I give him my sword for his rifle and it helps him along very much.

The Army is Heading for Pennsylvania

June 24th, 1863. We are moving in the direction of Martinsburg and learn for the first time that Pennsylvania is our objective point.

June 25th. Pass through Martinsburg about 11 A.M. and perceive at once that we are not treading friendly streets. The Yankee citizens feel doubly aggrieved since their favourite butcher Milray has but lately fled ignominiously through these same streets, having lost his entire army and only escaping with a small body guard. Late in the afternoon we reach the Potomac and being disappointed in our pontoons prepare to wade this mighty stream which separated us from our beloved Virginia soil.

Brief Retrospect

Terrible had been that march along the scorched and blazing plains of Virginia. Angry was the glare of the sun during those fearful days of June, as it flashed upon our ranks and fiercely smote again and again the burning temples of our fagged and fainting soldiers. Choking, blinding were the clouds of dust that rose from beneath the army's unsteady tread; parching was that unquenchable thirst which dried the tongue to its very roots. The men fell by tens, twenties, nay by hundreds along the dusty roadsides. Such days as these prove the true soldier, and he who falters not in the long and wearisome march will not be absent from the charge.

They Cross Into Pennsylvania

But now we stand upon the banks of the Potomac and prepare to cross. As we advance into Pennsylvania the road becomes almost impassable, so slippery is the mud; whilst a cold steady rain falls constantly upon our ranks.

Lee's Care for Civilian Property

The wheat fields are every where nearly ripe for harvesting, and all around plenty appears to bless the fertile land. We destroy nothing uselessly, but in self defence (on account of the roads) are obliged to cut a passage through these rich fields of wheat, which however is no larger than necessary; for our Generals are even more careful of the property of these Thrifty German Farmers than they were of the lands and houses of their own soil. And General Lee was so solicitous for the safety of the fences that he dismounted this morning (so we are told) and on the muddy road side made some of his staff officers assist him in putting up the portion of a rail fence which had been through negligence left down. We are further informed that several of the soldiers in the van of the army have already been shot by their generals for plundering the houses of these peace loving German Yankees.

State of the Army; and an Apparent Error

Never before has the army been in such fine condition, so well disciplined and under such complete control. Perhaps never before have we had a larger effective force, sixty thousand infantry with some two hundred pieces of cannon. (There are also from seven to ten thousand cavalry who should be with us but who, under the command of their dashing general, are far away towards Washington City, leaving our infantry and artillery unguarded in flank and rear, and stripping our cautious Lee of sufficient force to explore the exact position of his enemy).[1]

Dooley is in the Rear Guard

Our Division (Pickett's) is the rearmost, and we are left in the vicinity of Chambersburg to cover the march of the main body advancing on Gettysburg, to protect the convoys of horses, cattle, etc., the spoils of our invasion, which with very frail guards were being constantly sent across the Potomac; and to be ready at a moment's warning to join

[1] The reference is, of course, to 'Jeb' Stuart's raid, beginning at Salem, Va., June 25th. Dooley's strictures would seem to be just. (Cf. Freeman, *op. cit.*, III, 51–72.)

the main army whenever the enemy might be found, for as yet we were ignorant of his position.

In and around the town of Chambersburg we found the people very sullen and maliciously disposed, and not a few maledictions were hurled at us from garret windows by croaking croans; and many young but frowning brows and pouting lips we saw in doorways and even on the sidewalks. But our boys laughed cheerfully, and when contempt and scorn were shewn them answered by jests and witticisms rather than with the bayonet, as so often did those Yankee ruffians in our Southern Cities.[2] But here let me say that the inhuman barbarities and insulting ruffianism was not so often the action (perhaps was never so) of the veteran Northern soldier as of the low hirelings who skulked in forts and cities distant from the battle field and who continually fashioned their conduct on such leaders as Ben Butler.[3]

Feminine Fashions in Chambersburg

I was not a little surprised to see on the muddy road a nicely dressed young girl without shoes or stockings on her feet; and her companion, evidently a menial, likewise barefoot, being distinguished however from her young mistress by the size and uncleanliness of her feet. Here any where may be seen young ladies in silks padding along the pavement without *shoes or stockings*. Such sights are worthy of

[2] "... nothing but amusement [was] created among them [the Southern soldiers] by the Union spirit exhibited by some of the fair Chambersburgeresses. One young lady volunteered to deliver us a spicy address, ... which was responded to by 'Dixie' from one of our bands." (Loehr, *op. cit.*, 87.)

[3] General Butler was accused of having made large acquisitions of silverware during his campaigns in the South. When his admirers honored him with a plaque inscribed 'Benjamin Butler, Hero of Five Forks,' a Confederate wag added the postscript, 'And Lord knows how many spoons.'

note as manifesting one of the peculiar customs of this *race of people*, if indeed it be not a peculiarity arising from the war.

Sorrow Makes the Whole World Kin

A girl came to the ambulance where Lieut. Blair and others were, and told them with tears streaming down her cheeks that her brother had been killed in the 2nd battle of Manassas. And this poor creature had no idea of how many sorrowing and breaking hearts there were in the South.

The Psychology of Soldiers' Fear

*We know how straight into the very jaws of destruction and death leads this road of Gettysburg; and none of us are yet aware that a battle is before us; still there pervades our ranks a solemn feeling, as if some unforeseen danger was ever dropping darksome shadows over the road we unshrinkingly tread.[4]

For myself, I must confess that the terrors of the battlefield grew not less as we advanced in the war, for I felt far less fear in the second battle of Manassas than at South Mountain or even at Fredericksburg; and I believe that soldiers generally do not fear death less because of their repeated escape from its jaws. For, in every battle they see so many new forms of death, see so many frightful and novel kinds of mutilation, see such varying fortunes in the tide of strife, and appreciate so highly their deliverance from destruction, that their dread of incurring the like fearful perils unnerves them for each succeeding conflict, quite as much as their confidence in their oft tried courage sustains them and stimulates them to gain new laurels at the cannon's mouth.*

[4] This paragraph is typical of Dooley's sensitive imagination.

THE STRAGGLERS

Unpleasantly for myself, I am today in command of the rear guard, whose duty it is to urge forward stragglers and to keep up in fact all who desert their ranks under any pretense whatever. This is at times a painful duty, for frequently it happens—especially when the Division is moving rapidly, as today—that many soldiers leave their ranks through necessity, and, weakened by diarrhoea, can scarcely with all their efforts rejoin the ranks. Others fall by the roadside either deadly sick or pretending to be so (and who can be sure that they are only pretending?); others are barefoot, and although they may have thrown away their shoes purposely so as to have an excuse for desertion and straggling, still their feet are bruised and even bleeding, and it is a hard thing to keep these men upon the move.

FAIR WEATHER SOLDIERS

Many good persons during the war seem to have the idea that any man who wears the confederate uniform and hails from a confederate regiment must of necessity be the very essence of all that is truly brave and chivalrous; and they receive, as a general thing, all their accounts of battles and their knowledge of heroic deeds of war from men who, far from having performed the deeds of daring they so vividly describe, have never even witnessed the noble exploits of their brave companions in arms. For the true soldier has no time to stop by the wayside and recount his brave deeds to persons whom he does not know, and then devour their *buttermilk*, apple butter, and chickens in payment for the beautiful and thrilling tales he has fabricated. But he keeps in his ranks, is found in his camp, in the charge and the retreat, and leaves to the straggling coward the grateful task of glorifying his actions, who at the same time adopts them and makes them his own.

Nearing Gettysburg

Between five and six o'clock in the evening we come within sight of the town of Gettysburg, and are marched into a small copse of woods to the right of the road. Here we must bivouack for the night, for although orders from the front have been received urging our Division forward, still, owing to representations (as we understand) made by our General (Pickett) regarding the jaded condition of his men, we are allowed a respite of a few hours, and our part in the action will not be executed until tomorrow.

The Battle Has Begun

The second day's fighting (the fiercest portion of which was the storming of Cemetery heights) is now at its height, and we can hear distinctly the roar of the cannon in our front and to the right of the town. It is a stubborn and bloody conflict and we are sure if we escape tonight, tomorrow we will have our full share.

Dooley's Regiment Moves Into Position

July 3rd. Before the day has fully dawned we are on our way to occupy the position assigned to us for the conflict of the third day. As we turn from the main road to the right, Gen. Lee, or better known as Uncle Robert, silent and motionless, awaits our passing by, and anxiously does he gaze upon the only division of his army whose numbers have not been thinned by the terrible fires of Gettysburg. I must confess that the Genl's face does not look as bright as tho' he were certain of success. But yet it is impossible for us to be any otherwise than victorious and we press forward with beating hearts, hundreds of which will throb their last today.

How long we take to gain our position, what delays, what suspense! We are soon passing over the battlefield of yesterday, and the details of burying parties are digging graves to receive the freshly fallen comrades, and, in many instances, they have only the ghastly and mangled remnants of their gallant friends to deposit in these hastily dug pits. I pass very close to a headless body; the boy's head being torn off by a shell is lying around in bloody fragments on the ground.

So Frivolous . . . in the Hour of Death

A little further we take temporary position in the hollow of a field. Before us is a rising slope which hides the Yankee position from view. To the right of our front some quarter of a mile is a brick house near which one of our batteries now and then opens on the enemy who are generally ready to respond to the harsh greeting. Around us are some trees with very small green apples; and while we are resting here we amuse ourselves by pelting each other with green apples. So frivolous men can be even in the hour of death.

Preliminaries

Now Genls. Lee, Longstreet, and Pickett are advising together and the work of the day is arranged. Soon we are ordered to ascend the rising slope and pull down a fence in our front, and this begins to look like work.

Farther to our right is posted a division of North Carolina troops[5] who should have charged simultaneously or immediately following us, thus overlapping our flank (right) and preventing our force from being surrounded in that direction. Unfortunately, owing to bad

[5] Wilcox' Division. There was undoubtedly 'bad management' by the Confederate leaders at Gettysburg, both in tactical arrangements and execution. Considerable blame would seem to attach to Longstreet, although Dooley is apparently unconscious of this fact. For a full discussion on this point, cf. Freeman, *op. cit.*, III, 182–189.

management (I am sure not to want of bravery) they were of no assistance to us in the charge; and, advancing either in the wrong direction or when too late, two thousand of them fell into the enemy's hands.

Again, orders come for us to lie down in line of battle; *that all the cannon* on our side will open at a given signal, will continue for an hour and upon their ceasing we are to charge straight ahead over the open field and *sweep from our path* any thing in the shape of a Yankee that attempts to oppose our progress. This order is transmitted from Regt. to Regt., from Brigade to Brigade, and we rest a long time awaiting the signal.

Lee's Barrage

At last it sounds away to the right and the echoes have scarcely rebounded from the rocks of the mountain when the earth, mountains and sky seem to open and darken the air with smoke and death dealing missiles. Never will I forget those scenes and sounds. The earth seems unsteady beneath this furious cannonading, and the air might be said to be agitated by the wings of death. Over 400 guns nearly every minute being discharged!

We are immediately in rear of Genl. Dearing's batteries and receive nearly all the missiles intended for his gallant troops. In one of our Regts. alone the killed and wounded, even before going into the charge, amounted to 88 men; and men lay bleeding and gasping in the agonies of death all around, and we unable to help them in the least. Ever and anon some companion would raise his head disfigured and unrecognizable, streaming with blood, or would stretch his full length, his limbs quivering in the pangs of death. Orders were to lie as closely as possible to the ground, and *I like a good soldier* never got closer to the earth than on the present occasion.

Artillery Crescendo

The sun poured down his fiercest beams and added to our discomfort. Genl. Dearing was out in front with his flag waving defiance at the Yankees and now and then rushing forward to take the place of some unfortunate gunner stricken down at his post. The ammunition wagons fly back and forth bringing up fresh supplies of ammunition, and still the air is shaking from earth to sky with every missile of death fired from the cannon's mouth. Around, above, beneath, and on all sides they schreech, sing, scream, whistle, roar, whirr, buzz, bang and whizz, and we are obliged to lie quietly tho' frightened out of our wits and unable to do any thing in our own defence or any injury to our enemies.

Major Hutter tells me that he was conversing with a friend during the shelling, both having their faces close to the ground, and his friend making some remark the Maj. asked him what he said; and after waiting a little while for an answer found on looking up that his friend was dead—dead by his side and he did not hear the blow that killed him.

Get Ready, Pickett!

Our artillery has now ceased to roar and the enemy have checked their fury, too. The time appointed for our charge is come.[6]

I tell you, there is no romance in making one of these charges. You might think so from reading 'Charlie O'Malley,' that prodigy of valour, or in reading of any other gallant knight who would as little think of riding over *gunners and sich like* as they would of eating a dozen oysters. But when you rise to your feet as we did today, I tell you the

[6] In Pickett's charge the 1st Virginia Infantry was in the center of Kemper's Brigade (Weckert and Dickerson, *op. cit.*, 42.)

enthusiasm of ardent breasts in many cases *ain't there*, and instead of burning to avenge the insults of our country, families and altars and firesides, the thought is most frequently, *Oh*, if I could just come out of this charge safely how thankful *would I be!*

Pickett's Charge

We rise to our feet, but not all. There is a line of men still on the ground with their faces turned, men affected in 4 different ways. There are the gallant dead who will never charge again; the helpless wounded, many of whom desire to share the fortunes of this charge; the men who have charged on many a battlefield but who are now helpless from the heat of the sun; and the men in whom there is not sufficient courage to enable them to rise,—but of these last there are but few.

Up, brave men! Some are actually *fainting* from the heat and dread. They have fallen to the ground overpowered by the suffocating heat and the terrors of that hour. Onward—steady—dress to the right—give way to the left—steady, not too fast—don't press upon the center—how gentle the slope! steady—keep well in line—there is the line of guns we must take—right in front—but how far they appear! Nearly one third of a mile, off on Cemetery Ridge, and the line stretches round in almost a semicircle. Upon the center of this we must march. Behind the guns are strong lines of infantry. You may see them plainly and now they see us perhaps more plainly.

To the right of us and above the guns we are to capture, black heavy monsters from their lofty mountain sites belch forth their flame and smoke and storms of shot and shell upon our advancing line; while directly in front, breathing flame in our very faces, the long range of guns which must be taken thunder on our quivering melting ranks. Now truly does the work of death begin. The line becomes unsteady because at every step a gap must be closed and thus from left to right much ground is often lost.

The Turning Point at Gettysburg

Close up! Close up the ranks when a friend falls, while his life blood bespatters your cheek or throws a film over your eyes! Dress to left or right, while the bravest of the brave are sinking to rise no more! Still onward! Capt. Hallinan has fallen and I take his place. So many men have fallen now that I find myself within a few feet of my old Captain (Norton). His men are pressing mine out of place. I ask him to give way a little to the left, and scarcely has he done so than he leaps into the air, falling prostrate. Still we press on—oh, how long it seems before we reach those blazing guns. Our men are falling faster now, for the deadly musket is at work. Volley after volley of crashing musket balls sweeps through the line and mow us down like wheat before the scythe.

On! men, on! Thirty more yards and the guns are ours; but who can stand such a storm of hissing lead and iron? What a relief if earth, which almost seems to hurl these implements of death in our faces, would open now and afford a secure retreat from threatening death. Every officer is in front, Pickett with his long curls streaming in the fiery breath from the cannons' mouth. Garnett on the right, Kemper in the center and Armistead on the left; Cols., Lieut. Cols., Majors, Captains, all press on and cheer the shattered lines.

Just here—from right to left the remnants of our braves pour in their long reserved fire; until now no shot had been fired, no shout of triumph had been raised; but as the cloud of smoke rises over the heads of the advancing divisions the well known southern battle cry which marks the victory gained or nearly gained bursts wildly over the blood stained field and *all that line of guns is ours.*

John Dooley is Struck Down

Shot through both thighs, I fall about 30 yards from the guns. By my side lies Lt. Kehoe, shot through the knee. Here we lie, he in excessive pain, I fearing to bleed to death, the dead and dying all around, while the division sweeps over the Yankee guns. Oh, how I long to know the result, the end of this fearful charge! We seem to have victory in our hands; but what can our poor remnant of a shattered division do if they meet beyond the guns an obstinate resistance?

Defeat

There—listen—we hear a new shout, and cheer after cheer rends the air. Are those fresh troops advancing to our support? No! no! That huzza never broke from southern lips. Oh God! Virginia's bravest, noblest sons have perished here today and perished all in vain!

Oh, if there is anything capable of crushing and wringing the soldier's heart it was this day's tragic act and all in vain! But a little well timed support and Gettysburg was ours. The Yankee army had been routed and Pickett's division earned a name and fame not inferior to that of the Old Guard of Bonaparte. I will not attempt to describe. . .[7]

[7] At this point Dooley's original ends abruptly. Gettysburg had been fought and lost, and John Dooley had taken part in his last battle. During the night of the 3rd he lies in the open field with thousands of other wounded. He is now a prisoner of war.

Chapter Eight

GETTYSBURG AFTERMATH

JULY 4th, 1863. I have slept a little despite a steady but light fall of rain which has undoubtedly proved extremely refreshing and grateful to thousands of fevered brains and burning wounds. This morning I am unable to walk a step and have myself carried about ten yards off the road to where Col. Williams lies mortally wounded.[1] Poor Williams! He was badly wounded at the battle of Williamsburg and was a long time in recovering. He was a strict disciplinarian and on this account made many of the soldiers unfriendly towards him. His bravery had been called in question by his enemies upon several occasions, although none who knew him well and had seen him in previous actions doubted for a moment his courage. In the charge yesterday, foolishly and insanely he rode cooly and deliberately in front of the regiment, mounted on his horse; and thus the most conspicuous mark for the sharpshooters, he was hurled to the ground by a mortal wound.

(This was the second time that in a murderous charge the commanding officer of our Regiment had distinguished himself by charging mounted in front of the brigade. At the 2nd battle of Manassas Lt.-Col. Skinner of Baltimore, who had been with us since the beginning of the war, dashed ahead of the brigade, amid a storm of grape and musketry, and sabred two of the gunners at their pieces. The battery was won and afterwards turned upon the flying

[1] This was the officer who had placed Dooley under arrest (see p. 93.)

foe; but our Gallant Col. was disabled for life. His left arm was ploughed up by a shot, and another perforated his lung, from the effects of which he has ever since been a sufferer.)[2]

The Last Hours of Colonel Williams

Poor Williams! His spinal bone is broken, the shot, I think, striking at the neck joint and running down the spinal column. He suffers continual and intense agony. No position in which he may be placed affords any relief and he constantly seeks some change in the disposition of his head. There is a Yankee Col. close by who is doing all he can to alleviate the sufferings of those around him, and he most cheerfully offers to assist our Col. whenever he appears to suffer most. But Williams shows a dislike to be thus waited on, and frequently he asks *me* to give a more comfortable position to his head, which on account of the stiffness of my own wound, I am unable to do without giving him much additional pain. I make several of the officials who have direction of the ambulances promise me to have Col. removed to the field hospital where medical attendance may be had; and towards the middle of the day I have the satisfaction of knowing he had been removed.* I never saw him afterwards. He died after 4 or 5 days' intense suffering.*

Some Unfavorable Comparisons

A few hours afterwards, I am also removed and placed in an ambulance along side a wounded Yankee. Poor fellow, he is wounded in many places and appears to suffer very much. He is a coarse bloated looking Irishman and is whining and groaning continually except when the vehicle jolts over a stone or gully, and then he gives a loose to horrid oaths and imprecations. I long to get rid of my

[2] The casualties of the 1st Virginia Infantry at Gettysburg were 120, out of 155 men (Weckert and Dickerson, *op. cit.*, 42.)

loathsome companion and hail with delight the approach to the field hospital.

Although our men were all around me and suffering the most acute and oftentimes mortal pain, still I don't remember to have heard a single curse issue from their lips even in their most frantic ravings. Although the southern soldiers have the reputation of ferocious and blasphemous cursing, still I must confess that my little experience among the wounded of both sides at Gettysburg was altogether in favor of our men. That our men cursed and blasphemed in camp and upon the march cannot be denied; but, generally speaking, their oaths were the immediate effects of some emotional feelings, and whilst they shocked every fine religious sentiment of the Christian, they were very seldom intermingled with the foul and polluted phrases which gratuitously, like streams of filth, proceed out of the mouths of our adversaries.

The Field Hospital

The rain is pouring down as we reach the field hospital, which differs from the battle field only in this respect, that we have some kind of medical attendance and rations of crackers and substitute-coffee. But the accommodations are the same, viz., the wet muddy hillside, sans tents, sans blankets, sans fires, sans water, sans every thing relating to exterior comfort.

John Scammel is Sicker Than He Looks

The first man who attracted my attention upon being assigned to my position on this dreary hillside was one of the members of my company, John Scammel. Poor Scammel! He is standing up in his usually inert way, and wringing water from a blanket which he has been fortunate enough to preserve. There appears nothing very grievous in his condition, but he opens his shirt and quietly points to a piece of shell which is half buried in the hollow between his breasts. He tells me in a low complaining voice that he feels his time has come and that no one will by proper care give him a chance, if there be any chance, to recover from his wound. I bade him lie down and keep as quiet as possible and if I should meet with a surgeon that I would get him some attention.

A Night of Agony

The whole ground for miles around is covered with the wounded, the dying and the dead. Confederate and Yankee are often promiscuously thrown together, although the officials separate us generally as much as is convenient. The Yankees are nearly all comfortably quartered, having tents and blankets and many little comforts which they have of course received from their comrades. This is only natural and none of our boys expect to receive attentions in preference to the enemy's wounded.

A young surgeon is near me now, and after examining my wounds and asking a great many foolish and ignorant questions, I urge him to look at the wound in my man's (Scammel's) breast. He assures me positively that he will do so as soon as he has taken a bite of something to eat. Oh humanity! A human life or a cup of coffee!

This is a horrid night, cold and wet and rainy. Groans and shrieks and maniacal ravings; bitter sobs, and heavy sighs, piteous cries; horrid oaths; despair; the death rattle; darkness; death. The Yankees near me (nurses, they are called) instead of alleviating to some degree the fearful sufferings around us, are indulging in curses, the most ignorant curiosity, and obscene tales.

All night long I lie awake shivering with cold save when my wearied eye lids droop for a moment, again to be opened by a convulsive start as the wheels of the ambulance all but run over my feet. And the infuriated drivers curse and whip their refractory horses, or some yell or shriek louder than the rest tells how near the horses' hoofs have approached some helpless wounded wretch. All night long these ambulances move among us, still bringing more and more from that field of blood.

John Scammel Goes Home

July 5th. Morning dawns at last. Though raining still the chill of the small hours before day break no longer makes me shiver, and soon the carriers come around with their vessels of coffee, and this does much towards comforting the inner part of man. An officer (Yankee) is enquiring if any one here is acquainted with John Scammel. I tell him that he belongs to my company. 'Here then,' he said, 'are some little things I took from his pocket; he died a few minutes ago just a few yards off.' These little effects consist of a five dollar Confederate bill stained with his blood, and a paper showing the date, etc. of his enrollment. Poor fellow, he might have lived if proper care had been shown him. But our poor fellows are dying all around us and but little surgical attention might save them.

The Wounded are Patient

Here is a poor wounded Confederate who is walking up and down, wandering anywhere his cracked brain directs him. Just on top of his head and penetrating to his brain is a large opening made by a shell in which I might insert my hand. He walks about as if nothing was the matter with him, and pays no attention to any advice given him.

About two yards from me on the other side of the road is a Virginia Lieut., 24th Va. His leg is torn and mangled fearfully; it is now amputated between the thigh and knee.

There he reclines with his back against a stump and his wounded stump of a leg dragging heavily on the ground, clumsily bound up and portions of the flesh exposed and bedraggled in the mud. I have watched this officer pretty closely and although I have seen much pain and agony in his expression, I haven't heard a single word of complaint or impatient exclamation break from his lips. Only once I heard him ask of some negro camp attendant in a tone of piteous expostulation to make a little fire near him, for the night was cold and the rain was chilling him to the very marrow of his bones. No fires were made however, for whether it was against orders or the result of neglect, we suffered a great deal from rain and the chilling night air. My poor friend appeared to suffer so much that after a selfish contest with my better impulses I sent him over my oil-cloth, that being doubled up and placed under his amputated member it might free him from much pain and distress. This gave him much relief and he appeared quite grateful; and now we were both equal in regard to exposure to the weather, for neither of us had any covering except our clothes. *Long have I remembered this noble example of patience, and although I don't know what became of my Virginia friend, I have often recalled his quiet suffering form to my mind and described to others his unexampled equanimity.*

Thirst, and the Slow, Slow Hours

I begin now to suffer from thirst, for the only water they bring us is from a neighboring run which is warm and muddy and has the additional properties belonging to human blood and dead bodies. I have therefore determined to refrain from this nauseating and unhealthy draught as long as I possibly can,* which I did for four days, at the end of which I was so fortunate as to obtain some spring water.*

Ah, these days go slowly by, and yet new scenes are daily being enacted around us and serve to excite, tho' far from pleasing. The nights are far more monotonous than the days. Then the groans and shrieks and ravings of the wounded are much more impressive, and the wearied sleepers enjoy but fitful slumbers.

The Price of Battle

There is one poor youth near by whose agonies are frightful, especially at night. Both his thigh bones have been broken by a ball, and really his anguish is enough to move a heart of stone. The worst is that he lingers in this terrible agony for three days, and it was a real satisfaction to learn that the unfortunate boy had expired. Another victim and a member of my regiment is deliriously moaning and shouting all the night. He begins in a low tone of voice and shouts louder and louder, using only one phrase all the time, until he becomes exhausted. Thus he repeats frantically a hundred times at least the words, 'I'm proud I belong to the 1st Va. Regiment!' Then he stops and begins another sentence, shouting and singing until he is exhausted. Another of the 19th Va. has a jaw fractured and throat lacerated and is actually dying of pain and hunger.

What Has Happened to the Army?

Two or three days pass by and we can hear nothing reliable about the movements of the army. The Yankees tell us the most ridiculous stories of the hasty and disastrous retreat of our army, how large detachments are daily captured and how the whole will be destroyed before they reach the Potomac. But we know too much to believe anything the Yankees say, and know too well how glad these same gallant blue coats will be when Genl. Lee is agitating them no more and is again in Va.

A Few Aids for the Wounded

Genl. Lee, like the Noble thoughtful General he is, has left behind (before retiring) many hundreds of nurses (from among our private soldiers) and many surgeons of his army to assist and to care for the thousands of the brave men whom he knew could not receive the attention they required from the hands of the enemy. These nurses and surgeons are afterwards detained as regular prisoners of war.

The whole country has learned tidings of the battle of Gettysburg, and the nearest towns and cities are sending out generously medical stores, provisions, money, *preachers*, and 'sanitary committees.' The Sisters of Charity and Mercy are in many parts but as yet I have not seen any.

A Yanko-Irish soldier told me he was from Lowell, Mass., and that he had been a soldier under John Mitchel in '48. Having heard that John M's three sons were in the Confederate army he wished to hear something about them. He seemed much pleased when he learned that I could give him so much information about the Mitchels. And then Cronin [a wounded comrade] and I began questioning him and asking him how it was possible for him who had in '48 fought or intended to fight for the same cause for which we were contending, how could he consistently turn his back on his principles and for the pitiful hire of a few dollars do all in his power to crush a brave people asserting their right of self government; and now that he was engaged in the cause of tyranny, fighting against honesty, Justice and right, and moreover against those very gallant young men he was seeking to hear of, what, we asked, would Mr. Mitchel think of him?

The Power of Rhetoric

The poor fellow's eyes filled with tears. He said he didn't know how it was at all, but they got him to enlist and if he got back to Lowell he didn't think they'd 'get him agin.' He then went off and returned with two good blankets and a fly-tent which he insisted on our taking from him; and then hastily bidding us goodbye was gone and we never met him afterwards. Perhaps we were too severe towards him; but when we see the Irishman supporting so foul a tyranny as ever blackened the pages of any history, our indignation cannot but be moved, even though we know that he is the dupe of men who, leading him by the brilliancy of their talents, and trampling under foot their former principles of right and justice, rush madly in the paths of ignoble fame but to cover themselves and their dupes with ignominy and Shame.

A Tall Story and a Terrible Curse

In Mr. Maguire's rather partial account of the Irish in America, he mentions the fact that upon the march of the Yankee army to Fredericksburg (Nov. '62), as Meagher's (Union) Brigade of Irishmen were passing the house of the Mother of the Confederate General Ashby, a woman rushed frantically in the presence of the soldiers, her long dishevelled hair silvered by time and a broken heart, floating wildly in the autumn breeze; and kneeling upon the ground with her head thrown back and her hands clasped high towards heaven, she invoked in a shrill and broken voice the curse of God on the murderers of her son. Mr. Maguire did not and had no reason to relate what *may have* been the sequel to this frightful curse. In less than three weeks afterwards this brigade was almost totally annihilated at Fredericksburg, and (if I mistake not) was never after heard of as the Irish Brigade. The field on which they fell was at the foot of Marye's hill, and was the property of Col. Marye, an officer in our brigade. In 1848 or '49 when famine was inflicting such distress in Ireland, the whole crop of Corn raised upon this identical field had been sent in contribution for the relief of that starving and oppressed people. That people (the Irish), invigorated and under infamous leadership, have now done far more than the envenomed *puritan* to rob us of our property, devastate our lands, starve the pleading orphan and the broken hearted widow, trample in the dust every principle of right, and crush out completely our identity as a free people. For, if their strong arms and fearless hearts had not leagued with oppressors to destroy us, all the hireling Germans and money loving puritans that could have been dragged to the field of war could never have checked the onward wave of our victorious army or plucked from the manly brows of our citizens their wreaths of freedom and placed them with fiendish exultation on the heads of their ebony idols.

Dooley Begins to Feel Better

My condition is somewhat ameliorated by the kindness of our Lowell Irishman, and today, Thursday 9th, 5 or 6 of us are assigned to a larger tent and here for the first time my wounds are washed and some lint and bandage put over them. They give me no pain unless when I try to walk or stand. There are incipient maggots in them which further develop themselves in a few days.

With us was Lieut. Timberlake, 7th Tenn., wounded through the body and suffering continual and acute pain. The bullet had entered just to the right of the stomach but instead of piercing through, it had been turned from its course by muscle or cartilage, or something which it followed, and came out near the back bone. A Yankee surgeon examined his wound at this hospital and told him there were no hopes of his surviving over 48 hrs. Timberlake laughed (only weakly but cheerfully) and told the surgeon he didn't feel quite prepared for death and would like to live a little longer. The Doctor insisted that he was in earnest, and Timberlake (who had a very strong will) told him he was *determined not to die*. He didn't die, either, but for more than a year after that he was in prison with me; he was suffering continually and very painfully, for his wound would close only to reopen again. How well I remember his manly face with his long flowing beard. He was as gentle as a child and spoke most sweetly and affably to all his friends. But when wrong and outrage were mentioned, or insult or injury offered to himself, his high forehead would crimson to the very roots of his hair and one might well imagine he had a lion to deal with instead of the gaily laughing and agreeable companion of a few minutes before.

How patient in all his sufferings! For, though suffering month after month and day after day, he tried to smile and be cheerful all the time. I love to recall his high tone of honor and his gentle but sensitive manner. I recollect as if but of yesterday that I received some money in prison. He knew of it for I told him. He was unable to do anything for himself, not even to pay for his washing. He was suffering very much on this account and would not ask me to lend him a cent. I knew his wants and begged him to let me lend him some of my little store. He blushed almost to his very eyes and refused positively to accept of a loan because he might not be able to repay it. I insisted and he grew almost angry, so that I forced the money into his pocket and ran off.

Female Visitors

Such were our fortunes during the days previous to our being sent to Baltimore.[8] We had no little fun (in all our

[8] Dooley and some of his wounded companions will soon be sent to Fort McHenry, Baltimore, for further hospitalization.

misery, after this) and crowds of visitors were arriving every hour to inspect and examine in truly Yankee style, the wounded, and to see what kind of horns the rebels had upon their heads. Many came to assist in caring for the wounded, and brought clothes and blankets and cordials and medicines and what not.

Probably we enjoyed the appearance of the inquisitive (female) portion of our visitors more than they did ours; and had no lack of fun at their expense. There is the celebrated Miss or Mrs. Farnsworth (I think that's the name); she views all around her with the eye of a commanding general, and to hear the natives speak of her you might think that her sole coming was sufficient to heal all our wounds and save the dying from their menaced death. Miss Dix also is here, and condescends to converse with our party. This morning (July 10th) she spoke upon the harsh treatment of Yankee prisoners in the South, and *we* spoke of the tyrannical rule of Yankee *rulers* in the South. She asked if we had ever heard of Gen. Dix; that he was a kind man; and that no one could accuse him of cruelty to any one under his command or control.

What fun we have when the nurses come round to administer 'cornstarch.' About every hour a nurse of the feminine persuasion enters the tent and gives each one about a tea spoonful of this delectable refection. All take it just for the fun of the thing.

The Minister Makes a Slight Error

Another great source of amusement is the action of one of the sanitary commission who morning and nights and at midday makes the stations. He is a large fine looking man and has remarkably clear lungs but ruined by a terrible twang of the nasal organs. He rushes about from station to station (each less than a para sang in length), and dropping on his knees elevates his voice in prayer to the most high clouds and prays alike for friends and enemies for the preservation of the Union and the success of its glorious arms.

This evening he came rushing into our tent, half frantic, and cried out, 'Glorious news, this evening, boys, glorious tidings of victory! Gen. Lee and his whole army have been intercepted before reaching the Potomac and have been destroyed or taken prisoners.' 'Well, sir,' demanded our Col. Fry, 'supposing your news to be true, do you think that we can rejoice with you in the destruction of all that is dear to us?' The preacher looked mortified for a single instant, then a sudden light flashing across his brain he exclaimed, 'Excuse me, boys, excuse me! Really I thought you were *our* boys, and rushed in without perceiving how you were dressed. Boys—,' he said with rising dignity, 'I am *too noble*, too magnanimous (these are his very words) to insult a fallen foe.' He then launched forth into a self glorifying account of what he and the Commission were doing hourly and daily for the wounded, without distinguishing rebel from the truly loil [sic], and how the magnificent government of the Federal Union was going to fabylous [sic] expense in order to render us comfortable. 'Boys,' he said in conclusion, 'We love to heap burning coals upon the heads of our enemies, but we do not wish to insult them.' He then left us and we heard him crying his galorious [sic] tidings to more willing ears than ours.

The cause of this flaming report was the capture of a portion of the rear guard of our army which was rather dilatory in crossing their pontoons. We were however not a little anxious for the safety of our brave fellows until the next day when upon enquiry there appeared no confirmation of their magnified capture.

A Yankee Surgeon Minus One Finger

The Yankee surgeon in charge of all the wounds in these parts is a *Georgian!* But being educated at W. Point he has thought it incumbent on him to deny his native land and join with its enemies. He is a very fine looking man and has his hand in a sling, for yesterday when operating upon a gangrened wound, the knife with which he was operating cut his finger slightly; and he very sensibly (having no such wife as Edward 3rd had,[4] or if he had, she not being present) had his finger immediately amputated.

The Prisoners Removed to Baltimore

The next morning our party were told to leave Gettysburg, and we could go either to David's Island, New York, or to Baltimore. We preferred Baltimore, but rued our unfortunate choice very bitterly when we learned that every attention, care, and kindness was bestowed upon our fellow prisoners at David's Island, whilst we were treated worse than brute animals and cast into the black hole of Fort McHenry. We could not foresee this difference, however, and approached the Gettysburg depot gaily joking and singing, nor thought of the trouble and suffering awaiting us.

Jack Davis Again

As I am getting into the ambulance who should come up but Jack Davis,[5] one of the Sanitaries. Good hearted Jack! His eyes filled with tears when he saw me in such a miserable condition, for I couldn't walk without being assisted, and my pants were stiffened and caked from blood and matter. I am sure that if there had been time and oppor-

[4] According to tradition Philippa, wife of Edward III, saved the king's life by sucking poison from a wound in his hand.

[5] *Vide supra*, pp. 28–29.

tunity, Jack would have pulled off his own pants then and there and would have insisted on my taking them. But the cars were impatient, and after being tumbled into them like so many horned cattle, I was forced to take leave of my kind hearted friend and former class mate, wringing my hand and almost crying because he could not do something for me.

Chapter Nine

FORT McHENRY

SLOWLY but roughly in our heavy rumbling freight cars we leave the famous Burgh of Getty and, jolted till every bone and joint of our body was aching and craving relief, we arrived about eight o'clock P.M. in the subjugated city of Baltimore.

It is Sunday the 12th of July, and my 21st birthday! The depot is crowded by hundreds who have come to succour the wounded Confederates, and our progress has been intentionally retarded so that their kind hearts, so well disposed towards the enemies of Yankeedom, may be disappointed in seeing us; for as to permitting any of them to come in to talk to us or to serve us, that is out of the question. A rampart of bayonets excludes all assistance which comes not stamped with loyal brand and under loyal approbation. Many however come in bearing upon their best clothes the flag of 'our Union,' but judging from their sly winks and nods we are made to understand that the colors under which they are manoeuvering are not in accord with the feelings of their hearts.

They have lint and bandages, etc., and they have hot coffee and crackers which are most acceptable, since the pains of our wounds had by no means assuaged the appetites that within us were ravenous. Still these ministers of health (Sanitary Comm.) stayed not with us long, but like busy bees flitted quickly from car to car and we find ourselves soon in darkness in the lonely and deserted depot, and the only noise breaking the stillness of the night the heavy tramp of our bluecoat guard and the distant hum of the large city lulled to its rest.

Can we escape? I remember that Loyola College is but a few blocks off. But suppose we elude the guard? We cannot walk; at least I cannot, so that renders my case hopeless. So here we lie through the dreary night, slumbering now and awaking, imagining that same excruciating jolting of the long day is still continued and happy to find that we are but dreaming.

To Fort McHenry

July 13th. A wet dreary dawn is chilling us through and through when the coarse voice of a coarser guard awakes us to the consciousness that we must be up and moving; always moving on like poor 'Joe,' and like poor 'Joe' we feel, as we are bundled in every uncomfortable way into ambulances thereby to be removed to Fort McHenry. We are a wretched lot of human beings as, chilled by the rain, depressed in spirits and jolted almost inside out we are rolled along the almost endless streets that lead by the longest route to Fort McHenry. At last we arrive at the veritable fort.

We who had fondly been picturing to ourselves a large hospital were dismayed to find our ambulances halt before a row of low buildings which appeared somewhat like those in which I have seen cattle quartered. Finally after much delay we are ushered up a filthy staircase into a filthy loft. We are huddled together in this noisesome place, filth and vermin in profusion. It is the uppermost story of the yankee guard house of the Yankee garrison quartered here.

Col. Davis calls it the Black Hole of Calcutta. Our settling down consists in spreading our blankets on the filthy floor, and although many of us are wounded severely enough to merit beds, but one or two are given even *bunks*, and these are glad enough to leave them to their former occupants—the vermin. Cronin comes over to condole with me. Poor fellow, he can scarcely speak. He is wounded through the left lung not far from the heart, and moves about slowly, trying to be cheerful. But his misery overcomes him frequently. One of our Regt. tells me this morning that our Regt. lost all its officers at Gettysburg killed or wounded, only one taken prisoner unhurt; and out of 155 privates in action only 35 survived. These were mustered next morning by Sergeant Major Jones, who was in command of the Regt.

At noontime in steps a loud brawling Yankee Irishman with a large iron bucket of greasy [undecipherable] in slices and a pan of crackers and hard tack. 'Rations,' he shouts, at the top of his voice, and instantly the repulsive repast is surrounded by all the old rats of the prison house. but most of the new ones (us) sniff the air and decline to bite for fear of scurvy or something worse.

Wearily crept this our first day in the guard house. And the night, ah, the night! Mice and roaches gamboled round our heads, performing feats of wondrous skill to astonish us who were now in this dismal world of theirs. No pillows and no blankets to cover up, and then the vermin! And then the fitful sleep of the fagged and wearied wounded.

14th July. This morning it is announced that we are to be removed to Fort Delaware. Dawson and Sheppard[1] shew themselves very kind towards me, and in the evening when it is apparent that we are to be put on board a boat for Ft. Delaware, they procure a stretcher, and four of the prisoners bear me to the boat. During our transit—some hundred yards—I lose consciousness for a moment (the

[1] Yankee officials. Sheppard was a doctor.

only time in all my life), and when I come to myself I find an officer of a N. York Regt. leaning over me with something *akin* to *kindness* in his looks. I merely mention this as being the only look of sympathy which greeted me during my prison stay. These blue coat fellows appear to regard us as wild beasts, wounded, but to be kept alive for future sport or use. The officer I speak of remarked, "Perhaps he is too weak to be moved."

We are soon on board the vessel and very soon off of it; for some Union women made objections to traveling on the same boat with Confederate officers, and it being a passenger boat the officer in charge was obliged to concede to their modest request that we be put off.

Strange Songfest

'Back again' in the black hole, Ft. McHenry. We moan during the day and sing at nightfall. It is a strange thing to see a lot of wounded, miserable, half starved and melancholic wretches gathering in a social knot and forming a glee club to frighten off the more gloomy shadows of our prison walls. Imagination can do wonders in making one miserable or happy—'We're saddest when we sing.' Cronin sings and McGimpset is singing, and *both* have holes right through their lungs. This is certainly being miserably gay.

Rumors and Maggots

17th July. Raining steadily. Papers (which I never see) report continued serious rioting in New York. Today Sheppard who is most kind in his attentions to my wounds extracts therefrom 4 maggots and cleanses the wounds thoroughly. They are doing very well now; *I mean my wounds.*

18th. Gen. Lee is said to have returned to Va., also Vicksburg is said to be captured. I refuse belief in either report. Charleston is reported captured. I don't believe in any of these reports simply because they come from the Yankees.

Lonelier and Lonelier

19th. All the officers in the guard house, Capt. Jones, Lieut. Lee and myself excepted, are sent to Ft. Delaware. We are doubly lonesome now. I only find ease in lying on either side, and have become so chafed and sore that I am threatened with *bedsores* although I have not rested on a *bed* since I left my paternal roof.

The Wounds

24th. I suffer very much from my wounds, especially since the day is warm. 25th. Sheppard extracts from my wound several pieces of my pantaloons that had been carried into my leg by the bullet and which worked themselves back to the surface today, taking twenty-two days to go a distance of about 2 inches. Slept well.

Sunday Services

26th. Sunday. Mr. Hardy, Chaplain of 2nd. La. Inf. preaches today, previous to which we sing a hymn. And because no one in the room knew a hymn-tune but myself (and I only knew one *with a twang*) they prevail upon me to lead in the hymn, which I do under protest.

27th. The post-surgeon comes in today to see if any of us are badly wounded enough to be taken to the hospital. He looks at my wounds without saying anything. He is a grim looking Savage with red whiskers and Hoosier appearance. 28th. Capt. Jones and myself are removed to the Post Hospital, a clean and quiet building but not adapted to the exigencies of war since it does not accommodate (I think) more than 40 patients. Before being put to bed I am scrubbed well, especially as to my lower limbs; and the old skin from instep to toe comes off as completely as the slough from a snake, leaving me a *brannew* pair of feet and as delicate and tender as in the days of my infantine oblivion. I am now put to bed in the top story, with the tin roof slanting just over my head and the sun playing fiercely on its metallic covering. Now and then the heat of the oppressive July days makes my wounded members burn and ache as they never did before. Poor human nature. Ain't you ashamed of yourself?

31st. Heat and pains increase. The thermometer in this ward is about 92 degrees. Reading is a very unsatisfactory occupation under present circumstances. There stands a little clock upon a shelf opposite which goes tick, tick, all the night. I never saw pendulum or hands to any time piece work so slowly as did these hands and this pendulum. That clock is worse than the tortures of the Inquisition. Oh, what a long period to morning!

Heat today, Aug. 1st, 94 degrees. Every fibre and muscle are burning and throbbing. No position gives me any relief. Clock goes slower and slower.

Only a Slight Improvement

Aug. 2nd. Heat in my ward 98. But I am finally released from this fiery ordeal and transferred to Ward No. 2 down stairs where it is much cooler and where I suffer less pain. Several cases here of delirium tremens—Yankee soldiers. One in the next bed to me in dying condition. At night he raises himself up one time, grits his teeth and shakes his fist at me in most flesh-creeping style. Nearly frightens the life out of me.

Aug. 3rd. Heat upstairs where I was yesterday is 104. Just got away in time to avoid *crisping*. Delirium tremens companion is moved to another part of the hospital and dies unshriven and God only knows where he has gone.

All this time I am separated from my comrades who are in the adjoining ward in which there is no vacancy for me. Tonight I am wretchedly sick for several hours and nearly faint from excessive pain.

A Lack of Medical Knowledge

Today (Aug. 4) the surgeon asked a Yankee (Maine) soldier the question in three different forms, 'Are your bowels regular?' But the stolid fellow could not comprehend what he meant, and the surgeon, brutally indignant, told him that he could not do anything for him until he found out what his bowels meant.

A Friend from Richmond

Met Col. Lucius Davis from Richmond and played chess with him. He was taken prisoner near Hagerstown Md. after the Gettysburg battle under the following circumstances. The enemy were pressing them close. Gen. Lee, supposing Col. Davis to have a brigade of cavalry at his command, sends word for Col. D. to charge several brigades of Yankees charging down the road and bearing directly on their flank. Col. D. with about a hundred of his men dashed forward. His men stand and deliver their fire and then retreat, while Col. D., supposing them supporting him, dashes headlong into the opposing squadrons. He is battered and bruised from head to foot, his horse shot through the head falls on him, and the Col. is a prisoner covered with bruises and scars. He is very sensitive and very courteous. He is filled to overflowing with that idea of honour, good faith and lofty sentiment so prevalent in southern men who pretend to high birth and nobility of family.

Not a Dull Moment

Several more cases of mania-potu or delirium tremens, Yankee soldiers. One near me. Every kind of antics, carries on pitiably. He sees his child, as it were, drowning, and cannot save him. His wife dies of grief over the loss of the child, and then he places them in a coffin and has a large but most lugubrious funeral, moaning and roaring all the time. Now he stands up and beats his fist and head against the wall, etc. They put a straight jacket on him and drug him to sleep. Sleeps 48 hours and is allright.

Another one, an Irishman, is tormented by innumerable little blue devils and is continually employed in repulsing their legions with the open bible. Some times he reads a verse or several to them and cries out most fiercely, 'Do ye hear that, ye divils?' He also collapses under the influence of opium. Another tries to throw himself from the third story into the yard, as a brother soldier of his succeeded in doing last week, dying instantly.

12th. A vacancy occurs in the 'Sans culottes'[2] ward and I am transferred thither. We are all Confederates now in the ward. Enjoy myself very much today.

The Lighter Side

Aug. 13th. Every day now our wardmaster Cross gets us a pitcher of lager beer for which we pay 50 cents. Mr. Rosenberg (firm of White and Rosenberg), an old business acquaintance of my father's, works his way into the office down stairs where one of his *persuasion* (Jewish) is chief clerk, and sends me up twenty dollars and also a note from my uncle.

[2] Name given by the prisoners to themselves because the Yankees would not permit them to wear anything but nightshirts.

Boys Will be Boys

15th Aug. Cross, our wardmaster, attends to his duties admirably and looks very severe if the least disorder appears in the room; and I am sorry to say that some of my companions are not loath to annoy him in many little ways. Men confined as we prisoners are, by ourselves and seeing no company day after day, become perfect boys and are guilty of the most trivial and nonsensical tricks which appear all the more childish because they are perpetrated by those whose demeanor should be grave and dignified.

Capt. Jones and Lieut. T. are bent on teasing our Cross, and at night, pretending to be sound asleep, they begin to utter sounds of a vague and incoherent character in reference to battles, marching orders, etc.; Cross, ever on the alert, like another old fellow in the depths, rushes to their bedsides and by shaking them well, arouses them to an idea of what noise they are making. They yawn and turn over and nothing is heard for this night.

But for several nights they repeat the trick and finally agree to fix their crutches between their narrow beds in such manner that when Cross comes at them he will stumble and fall. Then they commence: 'Charge, fellows; onward, fire, halt! etc.' On charges Cross, but tripping over the crutches he falls prostrate on one of the beds; and one of the tricksters smothering his laughter under a feigned groan asks, What's the excitement in camp? Cross mutters an imprecation, and breathing direct vengeance if that noise was intentional, retires in disorder to his couch. Our good friends perceive they have carried matters too far and agree to suspend hostilities until a more opportune period.

A Generous Jewish Friend

19th. Mr. Rosenberg, formerly of the firm of White and Rosenberg, contrives to have an interview with me this evening. He is very kind and has furnished me with every thing I ask for. Nor does he do this from policy more than from sympathy, for my father is in his debt, and as things are going now there is not by any means a certainty of Southerners being able to pay their debts. He now asks me much about the battle of Gettysburg; for he says the people in Baltimore won't believe the reports about it, knowing that the Yankees always take pleasure in lies concerning their battles. Mr. R. has always been a liberal business man. He takes down a list of articles and promises to send them to me, and whatever else I may write for.

Leaving Fort McHenry

21st Aug. Today we are told to be ready to depart for Johnson's Island,[3] and actually are on our way hobbling and crawling, etc., when the order is countermanded and we pass one more night at Fort McHenry.

Aug. 22nd. The 'Sans culottes' abandon Fort McHenry. We are conveyed in ambulances to a large hospital on one of the public streets of Baltimore, where some 50 more wounded rebel officers are ready to go to prison with us. They are nearly all a bright cheerful looking body of young men, and, while some walk closely guarded, others among whom are our party form quite a strewn-out and long succession of ambulances. The people stare and would shew sympathy by more than signs were it not for the spies[4] that follow us every where and watch like terriers for the slightest demonstration of good will by the populace.

[3] A Federal prison for Southern prisoners of war. It was on an island in Lake Erie, about three miles off Sandusky, Ohio.

[4] In the original, Dooley has erased the phrase 'contemptible government hirelings.'

Tokens of Good Will at the Depot

At length we reach the northern depot near Loyola College, and here come the ladies and little girls and boys flocking around to see us off. Every one wants a button or some little relic of our uniform. The guards beat them back but the little boys succeed in running under the train whilst it is waiting, and they beg for the little articles so much desired; real nice little fellows, too. One must have a button for that lady yonder who is afraid of the guard; another for his mother, sister, and so on. The men never dare to act this way; they pass by the train and dare not stop even to look upon us, lest they be arrested and fatal consequences ensue. I am now sure that not a man stopped to look at us this morning while further north they would gather round us in crowds.

Chapter Ten

THE PRISON AT JOHNSON'S ISLAND

AND now we are off for the North! The whistle blows and we are whirled along, catching the last glimpse of the sunny South. As we rush over the borders of terror-stricken Maryland and enter the stolid regions of Pennsylvania every body of our party has his wound to shew, and but few of them have healed up. And after the excitement of our start is over we find it any thing but pleasant to sit up straight in the cars and endure the dust and fatigue of traveling in addition to the pain of our wounds. Still, there is a large fund of good humor and merriment on board, which I have never found at any time altogether expended, altho' it may at times suspend payments temporarily.

Arrived at Harrisburg we are entertained in a long narrow wooden shed with government rations and waited upon by negroes evidently of Southern origin; and one pointed me out to his companions as having known me before, but altho' I knew his features yet I cannot think of his name. I find my fellow officers very courteous, who altho' entire strangers, appear willing and glad to assist their more helpless comrades in any way available.

Scenery, Human and Otherwise

One of the most remarkable features of this country are the Dutch faces, and their eyes starting out of their heads, as if they were expecting to behold the great Andrew Jackson arisen and coming from 'Rebeldom.' Between Harrisburg and Altoona we behold some beautiful scenery. The

Susquehanna, clear as crystal, rolls its placid waves deep down beneath our feet and peering eyes; majestic mountains clothed in summer vesture throw their long shadows across our railroad path while the loud scream of the whistle announces Altoona at hand. Here we arrive by 1 of the clock in the morning, and pass the long hours till daylight dozing, cold, weary, and hungry.

Repartee at Pittsburg

23rd Aug. Arrived Pittsburg. A long wait in our cars in the depot. Soon after daylight broke upon this Sunday morning quite a crowd of the natives collect near the cars to have a view of the Rebel prisoners, and as the morning wears on the crowd increases. And our boys, who are always in for fun, putting aside the dignity of Confederate officers, begin quizzing in the most comical manner the more curious of our observers. Such questions I never heard before, and never waiting for an answer from the dark faced Pittsburgians. Our fellows poured into the ranks of the rabble volley after volley of the most ridiculous and taunting remarks. Some of the best cannon in our army had been captured from the Yankees, and as many of the pieces were made in this black hole of Pittsburg, our fellows took advantage of this favorable opportunity of thanking the citizens for the many and valuable presents of ordnance their city had so munificently furnished us with. The crowd remained undiminished until about eight o'clock A.M., when one of our party growing tired of their blackened and stolid appearance cried out from the rear of the car, 'Gentlemen, we feel grateful for your kind consideration and polite attendance, but, being very hungry, if you would only bring us the wherewith to break our fast we will appreciate your efforts far more highly than we can do at present.' This appeal had one desirable effect, altho' it failed in the main object. The crowd instantly dispersed, leaving scarcely twenty or thirty at a respectful distance from us, who bothered themselves no more about the 'rebels.'

Pittsburg Blue Sunday

And now they begin to move us out of the cars, up town. They try to make me walk, but finding that I am totally unable they are humane enough to put five or six of us, the weakest, upon an extra waggon, and we thus arrive at a large deserted hotel which is to be our barracks for the day. By ten o'clock we get something to eat—yes, something—some hard tack and bacon fried to *nothing*—and yet the officers in charge assure us that they are doing all they can to alleviate our sufferings. I suffer a good deal today from exertion, fatigue, and pain. Can see the natives coming from their Sunday worship. Perhaps I see them thro' a green glass, but they appear to me to be the *meanest looking* people I ever saw. The town is mean, dark, and gloomy.

At Last—Johnson's Island!

9 P.M., same day. Put on the cars again. We leave Pittsburg. Don't start until two o'clock A.M. Completely exhausted, I lie on the floor and with head on the seat get a few hours' sleep. Reach Sandusky City, Ohio, 12 o'clock, 24th Aug. People here less sympathetic and meaner looking, *if possible*, than in Pittsburg.[1] Get on a little tug and arrive about 2 P.M. at Johnson's Island, 3 miles from Sandusky, in the midst of Lake Erie.

Dooley's New Home

Here there is established a barracks and garrison surrounding an enclosure for Confederate prisoners and called

[1] At this point in the original manuscript Dooley has erased the phrase: 'No sympathy here, but rather derision and insults.'

an officers' prison. The garrison numbers about twelve hundred and the prisoners upon our arrival count nearly two thousand. But of these there are many privates, many hundreds of political prisoners and, according to the Yankee reports, several hundred spies, who, being separated from the officers, would leave about an equal number to our guard.

We are delayed several hours in a drizzling rain while each officer of our party is conducted before a Yankee officer and told to deliver whatever money he has in his possession, which may be taken care of for him and meted out whenever he has need of it. We are then all examined, and by the time this is over it waxeth late in the afternoon, and the orb of day is fast approaching that favorite spot of the great Lake wherein he is wont to take his evening dip.

Welcome to Prison!

We are now conducted bag and baggage to a small gate through which we make our entrée into our long inhabited and wearisome prison. Thirteen blocks or large frame buildings form the quarters for the prisoners, who, hearing of our arrival, have turned out en masse on either side. Such shaking of hands and meetings of old friends! Almost as soon as I enter the enclosure I meet Chas. Donegan (Ala.), a College fellow student. He relieves me of my satchel and accompanies me down the line, explaining to me the *ins* and *outs* of the place, etc., asking news from 'Dixie,' etc. Rob't. Y. Brown of College memory also greets me. He is also a Gettysburg prisoner.

For the present until I may get permanent quarters I rest me on the floor of 'Block 11.' Oh, what a relief to be at one's journey's end, even if the end be a dirty floor. At least here I can stretch my limbs and sleep, sleep, sleep.

How kind some people are! There is Col. Keenan of the 43rd N. C., an utter stranger to me and wounded. He hears me say, 'I'll go over there and get a drink of water.' 'Don't stir, Cap't.', he said in the kindest manner, 'I'll get it for you,' and with the greatest affability he waited on me as though I had been a long lost and long known acquaintance, enquiring if I wanted any thing else, etc.

Getting Settled

Aug. 25th. After a sound sleep the day dawns brightly on our new prison and Capts. Hutter and Ward, friends of ours, obtain for us a place with them in Block 10, viz. a ground-floor bunk, and make room for Capt. Jones and me in their mess. Our mess is thus swelled [sic] to about 8 members.

There are thirteen blocks or frame buildings within the prison enclosure, each one equal in size to Block 10, viz. about 90 feet long by about 25 broad, and having a ground floor and upper story. The buildings are built facing one another, six in a row. The room in which we are introduced is one of the three upper rooms of Block 10, each one of which is supposed to accommodate *very comfortably* 54 Confederate officers. Our room is about 30 ft. by 25, and has 27 bunks or beds raised one above the other 3 deep towards the ceiling, and each affording sleeping room for *two men.* At present we have 51 room mates.

Dining at Johnson's Island

At either end of the blocks are cooking stoves to which the representatives of messes repair in order to prepare the daily meals. When the meal is prepared notification is made to the mess, and we assemble around very unsteady wooden tables (in the lower portion of our block) for the purpose of disposing of it. Our mess having plenty of money live as well in the way of eating as we ever did, and I strained every nerve to enjoy the bountiful supply underneath which our table *groaned* and even at times *fell down*. But alas, for weeks my meals were a perfect agony to me, and I was often compelled to leave table and rest my suffering members on my bunk up stairs. . .[2]

Aug. 26th. I find a copy of 'Les Miserables' in the room, and as I had begun it at Hanover Junction I now undertake to continue and finish it. Some one told me of an old lady in Richmond who hearing of the publication of 'Les Miserables' concluded at once to purchase a copy, fully convinced that the volume was devoted to the trials of the miserable soldiers of General Lee's army, and being a warm sympathizer with the army she wished to learn the particulars of their suffering. Entering West and Johnston's book store she asked for a copy of the book entitled 'Les Miserables.' The clerk was at a loss. He has only one book that has a title at all similar to what she asks for—viz. a French work. No, she insists, there is a book called 'Les Miserables' describing the suffering and *miserable* plight of *Lee's armies*, and she thought it hard that the most enterprising bookseller in the city should not have a work so nearly relating to the miserables of Gen. Lee. Drying her humid eyes she is said to have left the store with every sign of indignation and dissatisfaction.

[2] For the next eighteen months John Dooley will be a prisoner at Johnson's Island. He now has leisure—all too much leisure—to make day by day entries in his journal, and to rewrite some of his notes concerning the past campaigns. By its very nature, his prison diary is full of repetitions. Each day was much like the day before, except when some unusual incident broke the monotony. Therefore, in the present reproduction there will be large gaps in the chronology. The editor feels that the eclectic method, rather than a laborious day-by-day rendering, gives a truer description of this period of Dooley's experiences.

Social Life Under Difficulties

Aug. 27th. Today playing chess, reading 'St. Dennis,' etc. Each one of our messmates takes a day for cooking and caring for the cooking utensils; but Capt. Jones and I, who have been admitted lately into the mess, are exempted from any work whatever, seeing our disabled condition. Jones moves on crutches and I find any great exertion, even eating my meals, very painful. This evening I limp as far as Block 11, being invited by some of my new acquaintances and friends. We have some singing, taking portions of glee songs that we remember, and after a social half hour or so I am compelled to retreat in obedience to the drum which just before dark rolls out a warning for every prisoner to betake himself to his own quarters. Five minutes afterwards if any one is found crossing the enclosure in any direction he is liable to be shot, and the ruffianly guard generally take every opportunity of practicing upon the defenceless prisoners.

Moral: Avoid Banquets

About a month ago (we are informed) one of the prisoners was wantonly shot by one of the guards, although at the time of his death innocent of any breach of discipline. The Sanduskians, it is said, were so gratified by this cruel act that they feasted and *ovated* the murderer; whereupon *eating too much* he was suddenly seized with a fatal illness and expired in a few days. (The truth of the latter part of the story *lies* with the Yankees, but at present perfect faith is established in the Narrative.)

The South and the Negro Question

Today Sept. 2 we talked of the Negroes. Some one told of the Northern lady who raised her dog to bite only *Irishmen and niggers*. And I may as well remark upon the word 'nig' and 'nigger,' that I never heard this epithet applied to Slaves in the South by any person of refinement and education. The Southern people, understanding the characters and disposition of the negroes gave them their proper place in Society, and insulting epithets towards their Servants were as rare among Southerners as they are common among their fanatical and brutal friends of Yankeedom and their hypocritical friends in England. Many in the South used the term 'nigger,' but it was a mark of the low and uneducated, the purse-proud vulgar, the stranger Abolitionist or the foreigner who was at a loss for English words. Excuse my *diversion.*

The Days Drag On

Sept. 10th. My wounds trouble me very much during these days. Weather very warm but changes at night.[3]

Sept. 11th. Very warm. Not a breath of air. My wounded

[3] At this time John wrote the following letter to his mother:

"Johnson's Island,
Sept. 12, 1863.

"My dearest mother:

I have been rather thoughtless, perhaps, in not sending you a few stamps, wherewith you would stamp your letters to me. [Only Federal stamps were recognized by the post-offices of the North]. I am at a loss how to account for my not receiving any news, whatsoever, from home. ...Tantie Jones, I presume, got home, or at least to Richmond, safely; I heard of him as in command of the Regt. the morning after the little affair at Gettysburg...My wounds have been healed about two weeks. On cool days I can hobble down to meals and walk about a little; but when the weather is warm I cannot stir around at all. The *leader* in my right leg must have been injured and it will be some time before I will be able to go about as was my wont. My health is in the best condition imaginable and we amuse ourselves with chess, cards, books, and *singing,* etc. etc. Where will Florry [his sister Florence] go to School this year? Alice I suppose has finished. Give my love to all the household; and tell them to write to me if it is possible to get Federal stamps...I remain your most loving son, John Dooley. [For permission to use this letter the editor is indebted to Mrs. Josephine Houston.]

members in much pain all day long. Try to read some of 'Peter Clancy's Matrimonial Misfortunes' but find them too dull. Evening: 'Island Minstrels,' (our prisoners' dramatic troupe) give a very creditable entertainment. These little shews [sic] are generally charitable and the admission fees given for the sick or more destitute prisoners. Sept. 13th. Another band of prisoners arrives. Gen. Jeff Thompson is among them. He is certainly an original looking man, and they say he is more original than he seems.[4]

Willie Mitchel

Sept. 16th. Chess, reading and writing. Dreamed for the fourth time last night that Willie Mitchel is still alive. Poor little Willie left France with his father, Mr. John Mitchel, to join their fortunes with the Southern Confederacy. Last fall they reached Richmond and Willie immediately followed our army until he came up with us, when he enlisted in our company as a private. He was then about 17 years of age and of very clear intellect and with talents more developed than is usual for one who had not enjoyed the advantage of early education. He had attended school in France however and was very assiduous in attending lectures in Paris, particularly those regarding insect life. He even pursued this study in camp, having a little manuscript book in which he entered all the discoveries he made with the aid of his microscope, describing minutely the figures and peculiarities of every unknown form of insect. We were nearly always together, messed together, hunted together with the faithful Ned (our Black Boy) and Tantie Jones, and built our shelter against the northern blasts which the latter days of November breathed coldly through our bivouacks.

[4] After thus piquing our curiosity about the 'original' General Thompson, Dooley says no more about him.

Willie would tell us often of his adventures in Australia,[5] of his long sojourn there while his father was held a prisoner by the British government; of the strange animals, gorgeously feathered birds, and strange productions; of his father's escape; how he was unsuccessfully pursued; how his mother and brother followed soon after and embarked on the same boat with Mr. Mitchel; how government men examined every one, and his father was so completely disguised that his family scarcely recognized him. Willie recognized him but his father threatened him so severely that Willie did not dare to do it again. One night on the high seas, as one of the gentlemen who were assisting Mr. M. in his escape, was putting Willie to bed, Willie asked very innocently if his father were not on board. The gentleman took him up and holding him out of the little window of the stateroom, held him over the dashing ocean's foam and told him if he wished to avoid a watery grave never to breathe his father's name whilst on that ship. So fearful were they that some little word or sign would betray the presence of Mr. M.

Brave and gallant boy, one of the color-bearers, he fell at Gettysburg, and notwithstanding all my inquiries I have heard nothing certain of his fate. And I have now for the fourth time dreamed that he is alive. Let us see how much reliance may be had in dreams.

It Is Not That Easy

Sept. 17th. Receive a letter from Fr. John O'Brien, Lowell, Mass. Generous hearted old friend! He sends me $50 and bids me get paroled and pay him a visit immediately. I write him back, undeceiving him in regard to the

[5] More precisely, Mr. Mitchel had been a political prisoner in Van Dieman's Land. He escaped to America with his family, as Dooley relates.

intentions of the magnificent government of the U. S., which has determined upon letting no more of us out of prison, either on exchange or parole.

A Show, a Shave, and a Story

Sept. 20th. Another performance of 'Island Minstrels.'[6] Startling event: *I shave my Mustache.*

Capt. Hutter tells a good joke about a private soldier on the Peninsula. Whilst walking up and down at his post he was accosted by Gen. Magruder (in full uniform), who asked him if he had not been taught to salute general officers. 'Well, yes,' said the fellow, 'I was told to salute officers of high rank.' 'How can you tell an officer of rank?' asked the General. 'Generally tells 'em by their coats.' 'Well, then,' asked the General, 'what rank do you suppose I am?' The man, supposing he was being quizzed,[7] replied, 'Well, Meester, I'd take you to be *about a capting*.'

News at Last of Willie Mitchel

Sept. 21st. Lieut. Kunningham [sic] puts an end to all hopes regarding the surviving of Willie Mitchel. The Ensign Wm. Lawson saw him fall just after his own arm was shattered, and Willie clasped his hand over his abdomen, showing he had been wounded fatally.[8]

The Staple of Prison Life

22nd Sept. Fine day. Yankees *admit* a defeat near Chattanooga, *so it* must have *been* a *rout.*

I have finished reading 'Great Expectations' and begin 'The Wanderings of Arthur O'Leary.' Am invited to join the Thespians. This new dramatic association wishes to

[6] Dooley suggestively leaves this item without further comment!

[7] i.e., teased.

[8] See Appendix I, pp. 217–218 for poem on Willie's death, written by Dooley.

improve on the Minstrels by abandoning the lees of wine or the glossy black of burnt corks and performing plays worthy of the intelligence and admiration of men of *education* and *enlightenment*. . .

Oct. 1st. Rains all day. At night several prisoners escape through hole cut in the fence. Long roll sounded and prisoners recaptured. The only escape which has occurred yet happened the last time the prisoners were allowed to go into the hold of the vessel[9] and bring away an armful of straw. One of these secreted himself under some straw (in a corner) that was not removed, and was borne back to Sandusky whence he escaped to Dixie, whence his friends in the prison here have heard from him.

Oct. 4th. We have great trouble to get water for washing and cooking purposes. Two holes in the enclosure have been furnishing us with drinking, washing and cooking water. This water being clearer in the morning we try to furnish each room with a supply of drinking water for the day; but after some few thousands of buckets have been plunged in these holes the water becomes troubled and muddy and may be used only for washing and cooking purposes. At present one of the holes is out of order, and all come down to our small well, which refused to accommodate all as abundantly as it did a few.

Oct. 24th. Cloudy. 4 books in hand now, viz., 'History of Ireland,' 'Arthur O'Leary's Wanderings,' 'Sir Humphrey's Clock,' and 'Old Curiosity Shop.' Pete [alias Lieut. Keiningham] gives us glowing account of how the wounded Confederate prisoners were treated at David's Island, near New York. The hospital was under the supervision of a regular army officer, who are generally as intelligent and humane as the others are stupid and cruel. Ladies without

[9] The supply ship plying between Sandusky and the Island.

number and gentlemen also visited without interruption the wounded prisoners, bringing to their quarters every kind of delicacy and convenience. They were permitted to nurse and relieve the wounded in almost any manner they wished, and even brought thousands of dollars to them which were distributed equally or nearly so. One poor fellow was even bored by their kindness, and, being wounded, a benevolent lady requested very earnestly that he would permit her to apply some cologne to his burning forehead. The poor fellow with the face of a victim replied, 'Well, ma'am, it's been done already fourteen times this morning, but if it will *do you* any good I suppose you may do it *again*.'

At night singing. Sentinel shoots at some officer and threatens to blow our brains out if we stand on the porch. Standing on the (5 feet by 3) porch is not against the prison regulations and this scoundrel is I suppose some *New England villain brainless* forevermore.

26th. Thespian Society give performance and succeed very well. As dinner was dished and waiting on the table, and Lieut. Burke brings in the apple dumplings steaming hot from the kitchen, the rickety table gives way and precipitates all the dinner in almost inextricable confusion on the dirty floor. Thus I lose my dinner, for I am in too much pain to wait until the debris may be gathered into an inviting repast.

Oct. 5th. Very cold and windy. Some rooms have no stoves, and officers go to bed, in daytime, to keep warm. Receive two letters from home, Florence and May.

A Doubtful Bargain!

Oct. 27th. Lieut. Phillips of 10th Va. Cavalry, who practices dentistry, desires me to lend him sufficient money to get the necessary implements to pursue or rather to start his business, promising to *plug* and *draw all* my teeth free gratis, for nothing. Have one of my teeth plugged by him immediately. Very, very difficult to plug.

Timberlake:—Much Improved; Dooley:—Fair

Today I feel well enough to assist in cooking dinner and supper. Whilst about making my coffee, Timberlake comes over to annoy me, and hides the coffee, then runs off. My chief occupations still consist in reading, playing chess, and indoor chat; for when it is warm enough to make a promenade up and down the prison enclosure I feel too much fatigued to enjoy it, and the nerves and muscles of my legs refuse to undergo the exercise of walking.

Remarks on the Copperheads

There is much excitement at present in the prison about the gubernatorial election going on in Ohio, the candidates being Brough [?], Radical, and Vallandigham, Dem. Much interest is manifested by many of our officers who favor the election of Vallandigham, because he is a Copperhead—as the Democrats are now called—and a Copperhead is considered an aider and abettor of the South. But we have done wrong and are still doing wrong to place any dependence in any of these Copperheads, who do not send us *arms, men, and money*. Arms, men, and money are what we want and are the sole instruments by which our independence will ever be effected. Give us these, gentlemen Democrats, and keep your kind wishes and knowing looks to yourselves. Captain Wm. Moore when passing through Baltimore as a prisoner, observed a fine young man *winking* desperately at him, saying plainly as though talking aloud, 'I'm with you Rebels, heart and soul.' 'Ah, my friend,' replied Capt. Moore, 'the Southern Confederacy will never obtain her independence by *winking*.' No, Sir, we must have substantial aid. France and England favoured us with winks and nods, and sympathized, as brave people could not help but sympathize with men struggling for all that is dear to a freeman; but France and England, the Northern Democrats were on a par as far as aid to our cause was in question; and the Northern Democrats proved themselves abominable and sneaking cowards as a mass. . .[10]

An Historical Parallel

Nov. 18th. Read today of the fearful cruelties perpetrated by the English soldiery in '98 upon the Irish. Their fiendish acts upon defenceless people we find sometimes paralleled by the infamous brutalities of the Yankee mercenaries of the present day. Receive a letter from Father, exhorting me to patience.

The Prisoners' Own Court

Tonight is Court night.[11] Boyd Mitchell condemned by the court to fetch several buckets of water for the use of the room. This punishment is adjudged on account of some little misdemeanor, and like all other penalties of a like nature is intended to relieve the following day's detail, while a breach of the law is also in some measure healed. I am appointed recorder of the court proceedings.

[10] Extract from a letter of John Dooley to his father, Johnson's Island, November 5, 1863:
"...You can't expect me home very soon; for really I have *so much to keep me here* that I cannot think of leaving yet. I believe the United States Government have made some alteration in the Exchange Bureau, and by the time the *swapping* gentlemen have come to terms I may be disengaged sufficiently to pay you a visit...You did not say if Ned [Haines] had reached home safely; remember me to him, also to Tantie Jones..." [Quoted by permission of Mrs. Josephine Houston.]

[11] The prisoners had established in their room a kind of republic, and punished transgressions according to their own law.

Nov. 19th. Sunshine. Read some, and copy off the rules of the Court for the government of our little commonwealth, i.e. the prisoners' room.

The shore batteries and gun-boat have some practice in firing this morning. I suppose they need all they can get.

Nov. 21st. One of my fellow-prisoners, Col. C. of Va., is the only Virginian that I have ever become acquainted with who could in any way justify the reputation of proud aristocrat attributed by some to the old Settlers and proprietors of Virginia. And he does by no means fully justify the character of an aristocrat; for, although he has many airs and is very reserved to those who do not know him, still he is very polite and affable when you become better acquainted. He takes much family pride however in his ancestral line, and from what I heard the other day I think he has been accustomed to look upon his poorer neighbors as rather below his particular notice. To explain: the Col's messmates are two of his own Regt., Capts. Robinson and Billingly of the 10th Va. Cav. Now it appears that when Col. C. wished to leave his quarters in Block 11, Robinson, although very slightly acquainted with him (not withstanding they were of the same Regt. and lived not far apart in Westmoreland, Va.), Robinson introduced our Gallant old Col. into our room, inviting him to bunk and board. Robinson does everything for the Col. in the most good natured manner, and helps him out of all his scrapes in the way of cooking, washing up, and *such* like; for which the Col. is not at all adapted either by nature or education. But Robinson is full to the brim with good nature, and this overflowing upon nearly all occasions he lavishes it in abundance on all around him, especially upon his Companion and Col. Now some ill natured person might say he does this through policy. Policy! Generous Capt. Robinson knows nothing of policy. His heart is in his eyes and his eyes are always twinkling with good humor, kindness and generosity. Oh, you should know Robinson to appreciate him and understand how such men can make even a lonely prison cheerful and bearable. Such being the state of affairs in prison, Col. C. remarked quite blandly to Capt. Hutter the other day: 'Really, I never knew how admirable a fellow Robinson is,' said the Colonel, 'and although we have lived in the same county all our lives I had no idea of what a fine fellow he was; I have written to Mrs. C., desiring her to call on Mrs. Robinson and do her every kindness in her power.'

I think the Col. shewed much simplicity in thus expressing himself, and much gratitude and nobility of character in regretting his long neglect of one of his neighbors; at the same time giving us a pretty correct insight into his wrapped-up and reserved mode of life before the war.

The Democracy of War—on the Southern Side

Ah, this war! How much has it done to lessen the distance and estrangement between the common farmer and the rich proprietor, between the workman and the mechanic and the rich merchant of the city! They all come to this field of battle commingled; the son of the rich man is in the ranks plodding along the fields, and the mechanic may be mounted at the head of the regiment. They eat the same rations and drag their weary burdens along the dusty highways, bound together by our common cause, to stay the footsteps of a dastardly miscreant race who, cowering in their comfortable homes, send forth fresh legions of mercenaries[12] year after year until it now has become a war of numbers and money; whilst every severe blow they strike

[12] Dooley returns again and again to this charge that the North is fighting the war mainly by means of hired troops.

at us is like a hemorrhage to a weakened man, and every blow we give them seems but a benefit, by bleeding them of their redundance of foreign blood. Whilst with us the distinction of class has been nearly altogether overthrown, it is far from the case among the Yankees; for among these the private is looked on with far more contempt by his superior officer than the negroes were among the Southerners.[13]

The Trial of George Bethel

Nov. 24th. Today the Court[14] passed sentence on Lieut. Geo. Bethel of N. C. He is to be reprimanded solemnly and severely, and Capt. Amington is to deliver the censure. About 9 A.M. Amington proceeds to fulfill the sentence of the court, and having arraigned Bethel before him, begins to administer in the gravest manner imaginable a profound lecture on the duties of man to his fellow men and of Lieut. Bethel in particular towards his room mates in general. The court had meant this reprimand as little more than a good joke, but Amington enters heart and soul into the cause and with flushed face and pointed finger overwhelms his victim with a raking and well prepared philippic. George Bethel stands with his plug of tobacco in his mouth, chewing away and scarcely knowing whether to laugh or to be angry. The whole scene was irresistible. The room was crowded and was convulsed with glee, and much of Amington's oration was entirely lost owing to the peals of laughter following nearly every period. Bethel is disposed to be angry but finally he laughs over the ridiculousness of the affair.

An Ardent Fox-hunter

Bethel, by the way, is of low stature, although he may be much taller, having several more years to grow. He is

[13] The observation, of course, is debatable.
[14] i.e., the prisoners' court.

stoutly built and very strong and active; young, thoughtless, he glories in nothing so much as fox-hunting. There he sits after lights are blown out and tells of his hunting adventures to his incredulous friends. He calls every hound by his name, gives their characters most minutely, their peculiar points of sagacity; follows them in imagination over the hills and through the glens, jumps from his seat in wild excitement and halloos them on, and only recollects himself when he perceives that half the room are laughing at him.

The Day's Routine and a Few Special Events

Nov. 30th. Very cold. Our plays 'Pochahontas' and 'Box and Cox' succeed very well although we (the Thespians) have had numerous difficulties in our way. Dec. 1st. Not so cold as yesterday. The Thespians hold a meeting today and we resolve to see about building a dramatic hall at our own expense, and not to play anymore on very cold days. Dec. 5th. Large box arrives from my good friend Fr. O'Hagan at Frederick. It is filled with nick-nacks such as overcoats, pants, drawers, shoes and even nightshirts and nightcaps. Good Brother Reilly of the Novitiate must have had a hand in the packing of this box, and my only wonder is that he hasn't sent some of his old stove-pipe hats which he delights so in seeing people wear. Dec. 6th. At noon characters are cast for the plays of the 'Persecuted Dutchman' and 'Family Jars.' After court adjourns and lights are out, Pete[15] and I go on a spree with one of our bottles of whiskey received from home; but we don't get particularly lively for we pass it round to a few others. We will keep the other bottle *against* Christmas. . .

Dec. 11th. Misty. Frost and rain. At night some officers from block 5 make an effort to escape thru' the prison

[15] Lieut. Keiningham, of Richmond.

fence in rear of our block 10. Two of them get through but the guard discovers the plot. The trumpets throughout the Island sound *to the charge* and the whole island is shaken with commotion. The officers who have failed to escape come running up to our room vastly excited and greatly chagrined.

Dec. 12th. Read Mr. Lincoln's message to his motly Congress—stuff! Minstrels perform this afternoon and get off some laughable jokes on the Yanks. The Thespians have concluded, all things going well and with permission of block 12, to erect therein a permanent stage for the production of our dramas. Dec. 22nd. Our plays come off in block 12. 'Family Jars' is a complete success but the 'Persecuted Dutchman' hops along on a lame leg. I fear our Dutchman has overdone his acting and in fact *played* himself out. Last night Gen. Archer with a few followers attempted to cross the ice, having cleared the prison bounds. The ice breaks and they scramble back to terra firmer [sic] and are now in the guard house nearly frozen to icicles. T. has a plan of escape for himself and myself. He has agreed to pay a Yankee corporal $80 and he (corporal) is to give the two of us the means of getting away, the attempt to be next Sunday.

CHRISTMAS!

25th. Christmas Day. Dismal Christmas! Alas, it is all the more gloomy because we can't help thinking of the loved ones at home, and the brighter the outer world, the denser grow our prison shadows. The hospital steward[16] promised me another bottle of my whiskey, but he is a gay deceiver and so goodbye to any more whiskey. Pete and I are determined to have something extra for our Christmas

[16] The author had deposited his whiskey for safe keeping into the hands of the hospital steward.

dinner, so we make a bread pudding of the crusts of many a day's rations and the remnant of our sugar, and have moreover *sauce a la bourbon.* We drink the last of our whiskey at night. But nothing can shake off the deep and settled gloom hanging around our prison walls; and nearly all of us sink into a dispondent [sic] and discontented sleep.

The Great Escape is Decided Upon

Jan. 1st, 1864. Prisoner Boyd tries to escape. He succeeds in evading the guard, but returns to the guard house and gives himself up because he has been overcome by the cold. He is permitted to return to his room.

When Boyd comes in our room almost frozen and perfectly miserable he is immediately surrounded by his room mates who must know all about his adventures. He is of the opinion that if any one can provide himself with sufficiently warm clothing an escape is possible, since no one outside is on the look out, the sentries keeping in their little boxes. And according to the Yankees the weather is *27 degrees below zero.*

The chance for escape arouses Winston, Capt. Robinson and Davis to do their best to gain their freedom; and although they have often failed before, now or never is the cry. A small ladder is constructed right away before lights-out, and they then proceed to clothe themselves as warmly as possible. Several coats are fitted to their persons; several pairs of drawers and pants, as many pairs of socks as will fit inside their boots and warm comforters around their neck and ears. Before putting on their socks however they procured from their companions some pods of red pepper which it was said would warm the feet and toes and prevent chill-blains. Capt. O'Connell, Tenn., of the next room, and Capt. Scales, Va., of downstairs resolve also to make the attempt with the party.

The ladder is about 6 or 7 feet high and they will have to spring from its top to the fence, placing it midway between the sentinel posts in the rear of the building. But how will the ladder be held steady for the last man to get over, and how will they remove it in order to escape detection, in the morning? Lieut. Thos. Holt White settles this problem by volunteering his services to go and bring back the ladder when they have all got over the fence.

The Break for Freedom

About eleven o'clock they start out, and all reach the fence in safety. The cold is intense and the sentinels are both in their boxes. The night is very dark but very still, so that a very slight noise may be heard at some distance. One by one they mount the fence and drop to the ground on the other side as noiselessly as possible. But the last one in getting over makes a slight noise. The sentinel steps out of his box and challenges; the prisoner is off through the bushes on the other side; and White, to create a diversion in their favour, rushes back to our room bearing the ladder in triumph.

He is pale and breathless when he reaches our block, and in turning the corner strikes the ladder violently against the house. The sentinel's musket clicks but Tom White stops not until he is safely under his blanket narrating the whole affair to his bunk-mate Haskins. The sentinel rests on his post, satisfied that an attempt at escape had been made, but that he has by his indefatigable watchfulness frightened the prisoners from their design.

Covering Up the Next Morning

Jan. 2nd. At roll-call (8 A.M.) there are three men present from an adjoining room who having answered previously to their own names in their own room, supply the places of our missing comrades; for the roll is called by room, and our room being the last of the block to be visited, and the prisoners standing in double row facing towards the Yankee, it is not difficult by entering the rear row to deceive the officer, who does not perceive the appearance of the prisoners as much as their numbers.

The Power of Example

All day the Yankees remain in ignorance of last night's escape, but at night it having been bruited about among the prisoners, our block is crowded to excess by the prisoners from all quarters in every imaginable costume and with every possible preparation, trying to do the same thing that was effected last night. But the night is less cold; there has been a slight fall of snow and the sentinels are all on the alert. Ladders of all shapes and forms and sizes are in requisition, but I think most of the attempts are futile; the golden opportunity has sped and Winston and his party sped with it.

Jany. 3rd. Last night the drains and ditches were at times crowded with men creeping towards the fence to escape. But the sentinels are prepared, several prisoners are fired upon, and one prisoner knocks down a sentinel and escapes. 5 in all last night are reported to have escaped. The prisoner who last night knocked down the sentinel with a piece of wood has been recaptured and ironed with manacles in a cell.

The Bad Luck of Captain Scales

Later in the evening Capt. Scales of Winston's party is brought back, and although he is suffering very much he is inhumanly thrust into a cold cell and told that he will not be freed until he gives information about his companions who escaped with him.

Jany. 4th. Yankee corpl. in our room this morning says

Winston's party stole three horses and a buggy from a stable and then turned them loose when they had gone a good distance. This morning's papers say that 7 prisoners are at large still. They must be in Canada by this time.

Capt. Scales is permitted to return to his block this morning, not being able to give any information to the Yankees concerning the others. Poor fellow! He was the last to cross the fence on that eventful night of the escape, and in getting over made some noise which, attracting the sentinel's attention, he was obliged to keep quiet until the sentry reentered his box, when he started after his comrades but never came up with them.

When he reached the lake he was unable to make any progress in the dark over its glass-like surface, being unprovided with woolen socks over his shoes as the other four had been. After vainly trying to foot it he finally fell upon his hands and knees and traversed a mile of the lake in this position. Having reached the shore, which is in this direction from the Island a kind of continent and not the mainland, his hands and feet were so frost bitten that he could scarcely reach a farm house nearby. Entering it he represented himself as a sailor out of employment and nearly frozen to death. Both parts of his tale might very well be true, or seem true, for he had been a sailor in his earlier days and his present appearance left no doubt in the minds of those who saw him as to the truth of his suffering. He was well taken care of, and on the morning of the 3rd the farmer took him to the nearest station on the Canada road; when unfortunately a detective not so simple as the good Copperhead farmer recognized in the grey habiliments of our frozen Captain unmistakable evidences of foul rebellion, and very soon Scales had resumed his captive fetters and gloomy prison abode.

The Prisoners' Spirits are not Totally Dampened

7th. A plan is formed by the prisoners *to capture the island.*[17] Today two officer-prisoners take the *great oath*,[18] to go out (as it is said) to assist those within to make their escape. Jany. 8th. Great excitement this morning. A prisoner in block 5 takes the *great oath* and the officer of the day coming to escort him out of the enclosure, the prisoner is kicked downstairs by his room mates and the officer is snowballed.[19] 18th. Snowing. Great snow battle. The six upper blocks attack the six lower ones. The first, commanded by Major-Genl. Trimble, Md., and the latter by Col. Maxwell, Fla.; after varying fortunes and many damaged eyes the upper blocks withdraw, leaving us in possession of the field, with many prisoners who are all paroled by us.

Indignation of Mild Major Winchester

26th. Jany. Some man who is called Hon. Mr. Ewing of Tenn. has recently advised his fellow citizens wherever they be in Confederate service to return to the *huge old bosom* of Uncle Sam and swallow the oath. Therefore a meeting of the Tennessee officers is held in our room today, and Major Winchester of that State addresses his fellow citizens in a *soul-stirring* speech. He denounces the conduct of the renegades at home as mean and cowardly, and declares that he and his fellow citizens shall be heard in their chains and their voices ring out through their native land in exhortation to the faltering to resist to the death the foulest of despotisms.

[17] Dooley makes no further reference to this remarkable project, which was evidently nipped in the bud.

[18] The oath of allegiance to the Federal Union. Release from prison would be the immediate result.

[19] This apparently weak-kneed prisoner (says Dooley a year later in his journal) found his way back to his Confederate regiment and was killed fighting gallantly at Spotsylvania!

Major Winchester to all appearances is a quiet and unassuming little man, but when he spoke today, his eye flashing and every nerve and fibre quivering, you would have thought that the strength of Six ordinary men lay in his soul. The meeting endorsed his views and a committee is appointed to reply to Mr. Ewing, if a possibility of publishing be obtained.

Two Significant Letters

Col. Boyd receives a letter from Major Winston,[20] who writes from *Montreal*. Feb. 15th. Receive a letter from Father. He says everything is bright and cheerful in the South and whatever suffering there may be it is not perceptible, but nearly every one appears to enjoy himself as though there was no war. (I suppose this is putting a good face over our misfortunes.)

More Rumors, and Some Relaxations

Every kind of rumor is afloat about our leaving the island by way of an exchange of prisoners between North and South. Feb. 22nd. In the evening we celebrate the 22nd by a few appropriate speeches from Col. Lewis, Mo., Capt. Houston, Va., and Capt. Fellows (Tenn. or Ark.). The Yankee officer of the day disperses the crowd, but not until we had paid the usual tribute of respect to Genl. Washington, the *Father of Rebels*. Mar. 28th. We read Gen. Johnston's report of the Mississippi campaign in which he shews that the surrender of Vicksburg was owing to disobedience of orders by Genl. Pemberton.[21]

Apr. 1st. I get off a good April-fool on most of the mem-

[20] Leader of the New Year's night escape party.

[21] It was charged that Pemberton, having been ordered to join his forces with those of Johnston around Vicksburg, had delayed the execution of this instruction. This deprived the Confederates of an opportunity to throw against Grant an army greatly outnumbering the Federals.

bers of our room by collecting their old letters and persuading Capt. Pitts[22] to deliver them when the mail arrives. Pitts is captain of the mess on half our block, and he is very much liked by all our prisoners. But one thing that some of us cannot bear is that Pitts when making an announcement to the room always addresses us as 'men' instead of saying 'gentlemen.' This certainly does not sound very refined. Today, read some 'Little Dorrit' and odes of Horace, some of which latter I bungle into verse. Have quite a mania for verse writing; hope I won't get crazy.[23] Almost daily a new rumor arises concerning the imminency of an exchange of prisoners.

The Story of the Unperturbable Sentry

May 3rd. Some one tells a good joke of Genl. Magruder on the Peninsula. One day he surprised a sentinel in the act of cleaning a musket. Every part of the piece was disjointed and the man with the most satisfied air was cleaning the lock with a feather. 'What are you, sir?' asked the General. 'Who, me, sir?', said the sentinel, 'Well you see, sir, I'm what they call a sort of a sentinel; and I'd like to know what are you, sir.' 'Oh,' said the General, entering into the joke, 'I'm, you see, a sort of a General.' 'All right, General,' said the fellow, no wise abashed, 'if you'll just hold on a piece until I git this here musket together I'll give you a sort of a salute!' The General sent him, I believe, to a sort of a guard house. . .[24]

[22] It is not clear whether this man is a Confederate or a minor Yankee official.

[23] For specimens of Dooley's verse written at this period, see Appendix II, pp. 219–223.

[24] Throughout May of 1864 the prisoners follow by the newspapers the confusing accounts of the struggle between Grant and Lee in Virginia. It appears that Lee, after the bloody fight at Spotsylvania Court House, is falling back on Richmond.

The Yankees have had Gen. Lee retreating for ten days consecutively and he shews fight every day at that same Spotsylvania C. H.[25] He must be a wizzard [sic] as well as a general.

THE RICHMOND AMBULANCE CORPS

May 7th. Receive two letters from home. All well and still expecting me home every day. Florence[26] at Columbia S. Ca. Ursuline Convent.

From some extracts in the 'New York News' it appears that *Pa* is chief of the ambulance corps in Richmond. This ambulance corps has been organized since the battles around Richmond in the summer of '62. It is composed of gentlemen of the city who are beyond the age for bearing arms and active campaigning, and whenever there is a likelihood of a battle in the State they are telegraphed for, and proceed immediately to the place, receive the wounded from the field and provide for them suitable quarters as soon as possible. They are of great assistance and comfort to the wounded, and frequently incur as much danger on the field as the soldiers themselves.

[25] For this campaign cf. Freeman, *op. cit.*, III, pp. 373–410.

[26] Dooley's sister. In the possession of Mrs. Josephine Houston is a faded tintype of John, with the following note in Florence's handwriting inserted between the back of the picture and its case. It is dated November 7, 1863, Columbia, S. C., and runs as follows: "My darling Brother is in Ohio on Lake Erie. I wish he would come home and come down here to see me. It would cheer me up so very much..." In the fall of 1864, when Sherman's army was operating around Columbia, Florence with several others of her schoolmates was smuggled through the Union lines in a wagon driven by her father, who had come down from Richmond in great alarm for his daughter's safety. Miss Coralie Lewis (Florence's daughter) says that her mother would often describe the terror felt by the girls as, concealed under burlap bags in the wagon, they proceeded on the eight days' journey back to Richmond.

A Joke? or a Sad Omen?

Some one tells a joke of Gen. Hardee, who, when he took command of our army in Tenn., found a great want of discipline and contempt for army regulations among the soldiers. This he strove to remedy personally, and visited the posts himself. Passing by a rough looking sentinel, instead of meeting with the proper salute he was accosted with a 'How d'ye do, general?' 'Is that the way, sir,' asked the general, 'that you salute your officers?' The fellow actually grinned from ear to ear and exclaimed, 'Oh, h——, General, that thing's played out long ago!. . .[27]

25th July. Today the order for the removal of Gen. Johnston and the appointment of Gen. Hood to the command of the Georgia army is read in our room. Grief and indignation fill nearly every breast. Probably no General of any war has been so continually unsuccessful (or, if you please, so devoid of victories) as Gen. Johnston, who at the same time has retained the almost enthusiastic confidence of the troops and generals serving with him. If they are in perpetual retreat they don't appear to mind it, and if they suffer reverses they do not appear to regard them as such. This same feeling of unbounded confidence and trust filled the brave souls of the veterans of the Peninsular campaign even when hemmed and packed close around Richmond in 1862. It never deserted his noble army in the disastrous campaign of Mississippi, and every batch of prisoners from his army up to the present have told the same story—that the whole army has the most implicit confidence in Gen.

[27] The summer of 1864 drags on for the prisoners. They receive scraps of news about the progress of the war, and most of the news is discouraging. Grant has not succeeded in taking Richmond, but the South's power of resistance is obviously and rapidly waning. The prisoners are loath to admit this sad fact, even among themselves, but they know it in their hearts.

Johnston as the man who is to bring them safely through all their trial, dangers, and conflicts. . .

26th July. The prisoners nearly every evening are engaged in a game they call 'base-ball,' which notwithstanding the heat they prosecute with persevering energy. I don't understand the game, but those who play it get very much excited over it, and it appears to be fine exercise. Another source of recreation to a much larger number is a quiet promenade during the cool of the evening. Then you may see hundreds of promenaders passing up and down the prison enclosure in quiet, pleasant, but melancholy converse. Their tones are generally subdued. It is more painful to look upon them than to join them; for, while we look, a melancholy steals over us and we think of the crowded streets and homely [sic] faces of those we have left in the distant South. . . [28]

Rats!

Sept. 13th and 14th. Rats are found to be very good for food, and every night many are captured and slain. So pressing is the want of food that nearly all who can have gone into the rat business, either selling these horrid animals or killing them and eating them. There are numbers in the drains and under the houses and they are so tame that they hardly think it worth while to get out of our way when we meet them. . .

Observation on Discipline in the Army

Oct. 27th. Gen. Early has met with defeat in Virginia, and his little army almost incredibly disorganized. The

[28] From this point to the end of John's 'Prison Notes' the editor has chosen to make very frequent omissions. The deleted material either repeats what the author has already described, or is lacking in importance.

cause of his disgraceful defeat[29] after so brilliant a success in the morning he does not attribute so much to the terrible effect of the presence of the magnific Sheridan, but more to the utter want of discipline of his own troops, who, instead of pursuing their fleeing enemy and inflicting further damage on him, scattered every where over the field in search of the plentiful and tempting booty offered them by the abandoned camps of their foe. In vain, says Gen. Early, I endeavored to reorganize them and lead them on in pursuit. Many of their officers shewed as little subordination as the men; and before any thing like discipline could be restored, fresh forces of the enemy arrived and attacking my disbanded and scattered soldiers drove them in confusion, but still resisting, from the Yankee camps.

Many here wish to accuse Gen. Early of being intoxicated, and attribute his disaster to this cause, but he has defenders. And upon the whole I think to any one who knows the meager discipline in the Southern armies, their spirit of insubordination and levelling of distinctions, Gen. Early's account will not appear at all incredible. The only wonder is that our armies ever do gain a victory, which may simply be accounted for by the greater ability of our officers and the indomitable *animus* of their followers; which, had it the discipline to regulate it that now prevails in the Yankee armies, would soon beat back from Southern soil the hostile invasion of a miscreant and mercenary soldiery. . .[30]

New Year's Day 1865. Gloom—blood—and repining

[29] This refers to 'Jube' Early's unsuccessful attempt to invade Maryland in the Fall of 1864, and his defeats at the Third Battle of Winchester (Sept. 19) and at Fisher's Hill (Sept. 22).

[30] Extract from a letter of John Dooley to his mother, Johnson's Island, November 27, 1864: "...I...wish to get as many of the Photographs of the family as I can because it may be a long time before I shall see you again...I believe if God will enable me to bear up against so long an imprisonment, he will certainly comfort you in my absence. My health

everywhere. All things appear so very dark and sad I feel like writing no more. Jan. 2nd. News somewhat more cheering for us. Jan. 6th. Trans-Mississippi prisoners ordered to be prepared to leave at a moment's notice. Jan. 9th. One hundred and seventy prisoners of the trans-Mississippi department (captured at Port Hudson and Vicksburg) left today. for exchange. This is cheering indeed; for, although they are returning where the Confederacy has long been asleep and a dead weight, it gives us some hope that they will not be the only ones who may be exchanged and once having set the ball in motion we may all be rolled to our homes. . .

22nd Jany. *For the 189th time* we are all exchanged and will leave in a few days for Dixie. The whole prison is in an uproar, for the papers have said it. . . . There is continual suffering among the prisoners. Many go to the slop barrels and garbage piles to gather from the refuse a handful of revolting food. Such is the infamous government we have to deal with, and now I do not wonder if we be overcome in the end. . .[31]

---

is very good and I am stronger than I was when I left home. I often long to be with you all; but perhaps it is better not to think of home until we shall be on our way thither...Write often to your loving Son, John Dooley." Courtesy of Mrs. Josephine Houston.

[31] At about this time another of John's fellow prisoners—Captain J. P. Hutter, was released; and he carried with him to Richmond one of the author's notebooks, with the following message written on the flyleaf:

'Memoranda, Jan. 27, '65, Johnson's Island.

'I, J.E.D., am in the best of health. Weigh 112 lbs. exactly. Would like to get all the assistance from my friends in South that it is possible for them to render me. Provisions and money very acceptable. I am improving my time a little, as much as I can, surrounded as I am by so many and distressing circumstances. I never get letters from home, owing to the interruption of the mails. I will write as soon as I shall hear from any of you at home. Capt. Hutter will give you this book. Love to all and write often to me. J.E.D.'

For the opportunity of seeing this book the editor is indebted to Mrs. Josephine Houston.

Feb. 16. The excitement is growing intense. 120 prisoners leave today. They will leave according to States. Those from *free* States have preference of being freed before the others. . .

Feb. 19. The May and June prisoners (those captured in May and June '63) are to leave tomorrow. Charley Donegan goes among them. Poor Charley was deep in the blues yesterday. He should have gone with the last batch but his name was accidentally overlooked and he was left behind. But he is hopeful today, being promised for certain to be among the next that go. He takes a book to Sister for me, and says that he will visit the home folk and tell them to be of good cheer, that I am coming too. He will no doubt tell them also his mouse story, viz., that one night it was so cold in his room in block 2 that a little mouse starting from its hole to run across the floor, was unable to complete its journey and *expired* frozen to *death* in the *middle of the room.* God speed you, Charley Donegan, with good news to our anxious friends. . .

21st. Another squad of one hundred left yesterday. There is in block 5 an artist photographer who takes pictures for 50 cents each; and because I *feel so good* I determined I shall not leave this dreary old isle without expending the enormous sum of fifty cents upon a photograph which I shall send to one of the warmest friends I have on earth, viz., Fr. O'Hagan, S.J. So with my bushy hair in no very neat order, and with Haskins' double-breasted coat (quarter of a mile too large) I march off to the Photographer, fully determined to let him do his worst. The good fellow who is to take our pictures is one of us, and has his establishment near the roof of the building.

First we ascend a ladder nailed against the side of the house, and after reaching the rafters we crawl from one to another until we reach a kind of platform made of boards laid loosely over the rafters and joists. All the instruments that the prisoner uses he has made himself while in prison, and all he gets from the Yankees is a little coloring. There is just sufficient light and no more, but notwithstanding all the disadvantages under which he labours he succeeds in taking very correct pictures; and if they are rough, certainly he has rough subjects to delineate. I am very well satisfied with mine, and send it off to Fr. O'Hagan as a sample of a rebel prisoner on Johnson's Island. . .

Chapter Eleven

PAROLED! AND HOME!

FEB. 27. *Two hundred prisoners leave and one hundred more to go today and I am among the number*—GLORY ALLELUIA!. . .

We get the order to be ready only about 9 A.M.[1] and are expected to leave about the middle of the day. So many little things to be packed up and affairs to be settled! So many to tell goodbye to! I feel head over heels in confusion and scarcely know which way to turn first.

Lieut. Kunningham my bed-mate[2] is almost as much excited as myself and in order to relieve me of some of my embarrassment actually takes the pair of shoes I intend to wear on my journey and *blackens them nicely* for me. Pete has no pride about such things and provided it is for a friend and honorable he cares not what he does.

An Ill-chosen Partner

Everything packed up and arranged, we must go to the officials and report. In going out I lock arms with Capt. —— of Tenn., *six feet five inches* in his socks.[3] And many are the jokes cracked upon us two as we make our way through the Yankee guard; such as, 'There goes father and son,'

[1] Under guard the Confederate prisoners were to be transported to Richmond, where they would be deposited in exchange for an equal number of Federals released by the South.

[2] Keiningham must wait several more weeks before securing his freedom.

[3] Dooley was about five feet seven inches in height.

'Big one and little one,' etc. But we are too much overjoyed to notice their little railleries. . .

The lake is frozen over to Sandusky, a space of 3 miles.[4] The ice is like glass and not very strong in some places. Some of the more Southern prisoners have never walked on ice before today, and, like cattle when for the first time they are urged to enter a steamboat, refuse at first to trust their feet to the slippery surface of the lake. Finally all are embarked, but no sooner have they taken a half dozen steps than there are some half dozen falls; and the poor bewildered fellows are almost tempted to return to prison, so great is the danger of breaking their necks.

Many others had very sensibly covered their shoes with flannel socks and are getting along famously. Others not being able to keep on their legs at all sit down on the ice and get their companions to pull them along. But it soon becomes evident that this mode of proceeding has its very serious inconveniences, and that if they do not change their *base of operations* they will arrive at Sandusky minus a considerable portion of their nether garments.

The Three Unsympathetic Damsels

When about half way to Sandusky several young damsels (three) in company with their father skate towards us. They follow us for some distance, regarding our party with characteristic impertinence and *wishing* that some of us would fall, so as to have a laugh at our expense. I wouldn't fall for anything now, but come very near it several times. I believe only one had the mortification of gratifying these strangers by elevating his heels in the air and bumping his head on the ice.

[4] The paroled men will be led across the lake to the railroad depot at Sandusky.

And now over two hundred of us are strung out for over a mile on the ice. At last we are on the dirty shore of Sandusky. It is the meanest town (except Pittsburg) I ever entered. . . . We go by rail from Sandusky through Pittsburg and Harrisburg to Baltimore, which we reach on Feb. 28th. . .

We begin our march through some of the principal streets of Baltimore. The highest windows of the houses are crowded with partially-seen forms, many a handkerchief and nightcap is waved suddenly and mysteriously from half open windows. The men, as upon former occasions, are afraid to take more than a hasty glance at us, and even the ladies, they say, are in imminent danger whenever they shew sympathy of the slightest description to their jaded and war-worn countrymen. We are assured as a positive fact, that the day before yesterday the daughter of a prominent citizen was run through by the bayonet of a ruffianly hireling for shewing sympathy towards a number of Confederates returning to their homes.

IT *IS* SO GOOD TO BE NEARING HOME!

As we turn into one of the principal streets, a sudden enthusiasm, like a magnetic shock, runs through the entire body of our seven hundred,[5] and an universal shout of exultation pealed through the streets of Baltimore. The little popinjay of a fellow in charge of our guard became frantic at this demonstration and threatened us with the severest punishments if any similar exhibition of feeling was evinced. But he was answered with derisive laughter, and vented his fury upon his guard by bidding them in insolent

[5] It is not clear from Dooley's account how the original number of prisoners became so large. There will be 1100 before they reach Richmond.

language to see that the prisoners behaved themselves in future. . .

At 1 P.M., February 28, we leave Baltimore on the steamer 'Cambria,' bound for Richmond. We are now 1100 prisoners in all. In the early morning of March 1, we have our first glimpse of our homeland. . .

We pass Fortress Monroe. Hampton Roads we find crowded with every description of ship, and we are soon moving slowly up our own little James. We almost hold our breath as we glide along its yellow waves and are borne in triumph towards our native land.

On either shore reigns the stillness of desolation, and soft murmuring waves sound sad to the ears which heard them in happier times. The landing places are destroyed and charred ruins of happy homes meet the eye on every side. The habitations that remain shew but little signs of life, but look mournfully down upon devastated fields and desecrated graves. Alas, the envious invader has not spared Virginia's pride, and heavy has been the tread of war's iron heel, and the blight of the destroyer has withered the land. . .

We are gliding towards the landing;[6] delightful thought! Our boat is now along side of one which only arrived a few hours ago, bearing sick and *dead* Confederates. Alas, poor fellows, what suffering! And many were not even allowed to catch sight of their own dear Dixie before death claimed them for his own. About twenty lie on this boat, faces covered and their spirits fled. Many others will die before they reach Richmond, and others will have only the mournful satisfaction of dying in hospital in the capital of the Confederacy. Their sunken and glazed eyes attest this, and

[6] Aiken's Landing, the designated place for the exchange of prisoners. This is the big moment of the journey.

their strong hope that something may yet be done for them in Dixie is all that stops the clutch of death pressing upon their throats.

Poor fellows! Poor fellows! How anxious they are to reach once more Southern soil. See! the most emaciated among them spring forward with a light step as if they could walk for miles in such a cause; but exhausted by their efforts they fall prostrate and have to be conveyed in ambulances or whatever vehicles can be furnished. It is pitiable to see these pale faces and emaciated limbs enlivened by sudden and superhuman energies and pressing forward to make the wearisome journey of 4 miles which must be made before we reach our boat sixteen miles from Richmond.[7]

Home at Last

The roads are heavy from the recent rains, and, unaccustomed to walking, we find it as much as we can do not to break down. Crowds of recently freed negroes stop their work in the fortifications off the roads, and hasten with pick and shovel in hand to gaze upon their former masters. Poor fellows! A change of masters is not always the best.

At last we reach our flag-of-truce boat which we take possession of with deafening cheers. My brother James[8] is among the first to hail me and bid me welcome, being one of the Committee to look after the wounded.

We are moving on towards Richmond-town where we arrive a little before dark. My brother and I proceed together to the house where to a surety there is great rejoicing over the long lost prisoner. Thus have I returned after an absence of 21 months, 20 of which I have spent in prison.

[7] Evidently a portage, so to speak, had to be made from Aiken's Landing to a point four miles distant, where another boat would be taken to cover the remaining sixteen miles to Richmond.

[8] Major James Dooley, later the great civic benefactor of Richmond.

Morale is Low in Richmond

The returned prisoners are far more hopeful than the citizens and those who have remained at home watching the coming events with anxious scrutiny. I find nearly all my friends gloomy and despondent in regard to the future of the Confederacy. Several causes combine especially to cause this gloom; among which I may enumerate the contraction of the limits of the Confederacy, the late dispersion of Early's last remnants of a force in the Valley, the difficulty to provide sufficient rations for the soldiers, the frequent desertions from our ranks; and another cause slight but often weighing much upon the spirits is that the weather has been raining and gloomy for some time past. . .[9]

March 6th. Make several calls. Spend much paper money. Draw my pay for 6 months as Capt., $780. And a common pair of shoes costs me $350; good boots are from $800 to $1500 a pair. A pound of candy is $17; an apple of good size $4; hats from $150 to $700 apiece; a wiskey [sic] straight $5, a mixed drink $10. Wonderful prices! So that two pair of shoes exhaust a captain's pay for six months. Flour is from $1000 to $1500 per barrel. Tobacco is quite cheap, being only $20 or $25 a plug. It is issued now as rations to the soldiers, whose pay, I believe, amounts to about $17 a month.

A Quiet 17th of March, Not Without a Hitch

St. Patrick's Day. At night attend church. Upon returning home we find some company awaiting Pa's appearance, who having invited them forgot it and went to church. Having partaken of wine and apple brandy in honour of the Day, and having quite a social evening we retire to rest.

[9] Until the end of March Dooley will stay in Richmond, with a few brief visits to his old regiment, now encamped near Petersburg.

Consoling the Colonel

25th. At night Jones and I pay a visit to Col. Lucius Davis at the Lawrence House. We take some wine with him and have a long chat. He considers that the greatest injustice has been done him by the government raising to high positions young and inexperienced officers (and even placing his inferiors above him in his own brigade), while he has been left with the same rank he obtained in the beginning of the war. For these and other reasons he has resigned his commission. He is no doubt a gallant and courteous soldier and gentleman, was a classmate of General Lee at W. Point; and he says that Genl. Lee wrote to him most kindly, sympathizing with him and promising to do all in his power to give him a position suitable to his talents and deserts.

Chapter Twelve

A TRIP THROUGH THE SOUTH: SPRING, 1865

MARCH 30th, 1865. Ben Haskins and I having agreed upon a visit to Ben Brown at Amherst C.H., begin our journey this morning. . .[1]

We go from Danville to Burkeville Junction, where we must stay over night before catching the next train for Lynchburg. While we are here an alarm is raised that the Yankee cavalry are coming over the hills to attack the town. . .

The enemy are even seen, by those most alarmed, and pointed out drawn up in line of battle upon an elevated range of hills a mile or two distant. Their movements, too, may be indistinctly observed and an onset with sabres drawn, might be momentarily expected. But an old resident of Burkeville was certain that he had *seen them trees standing thar* ever since he could remember! So that our alarmists after all in getting up this panic had only Quixotic premises for their basis. The trees continue to move their arms and shake their leafy plumes, but as they do not charge us with sword or lance our fears gradually subside.

[1] There was, it would seem, in John Dooley a strain of restlessness; it may have been a leaning towards adventure. At any rate, towards the end of March he was eager to be on the move again. His parole status gave him the privilege of passing through the Federal lines in sectors not the scene of actual battle. He was anxious to penetrate farther South, to see what was happening to the waning fortunes of the Confederacy. On the 30th, therefore, he and his friend Ben Haskins begin their journey, with the half-excuse of visiting a comrade at Amherst Court House. He did not realize that he was undertaking a trip which would bring him face to face with the stark tragedy of the South at the very moment of Lee's surrender at Appomattox.

A Rather Pointed Remark

While partaking of our supper at the hotel I notice the big buck negro (attending us) staring very hard at me and evidently amused. 'What are you grinning at, boy?' said I, half in earnest, half in joke; upon which the fellow laughed out and cried, 'Golly, massa! You'se the littlest cap'n I ever seed!' Ben laughed and I laughed; for although I am not so low in statue [sic] as some others of my acquaintance, still, height, breadth, etc. combined, I suppose I am pretty small in the eyes of others. Supping lightly we slept heavily, nor awaked till the golden beams of the rising sun burst into our room and darted under our eyelids. . .

We reach Amherst C. H., and are welcomed by the Browns. . .

While at dinner at the Browns' one of Brown's servants, just arrived from Lynchburg, reports the fall and capture of Richmond by the Yankees. Of course that's all nonsense! Can't *fool me* like that. I've heard of Richmond being taken too often to believe any such rumour as that! But suppose there should be truth in the rumour? Just supposing now Richmond has been captured; what on the face of the earth am I to do? Cut off from home; no money; no clothes; the very thought is distracting; no, no, it cannot be so. . . .

The Tragic Truth

Reach Lynchburg 6 P.M. Richmond is beyond doubt the prize of the enemy. It is no longer in doubt. Live persons are here who beheld the exulting Yankee enter her burning streets. Great God, then it is too true! This intelligence is the most afflicting I ever received. I feel bewildered, crushed, by the sudden, fearful fall. Never before have I felt so desolate, so prostrate, so hopeless. Farewell, poor burning Richmond! Oh, that whole seas of blood and treasure, poured out in your defence, should be rendered of no avail by the disaster of a single day! No more to see my sisters and mother! And where shall I look for Father and Brother? Where is the old First, and *bloody First*, as Gen. Kemper styled us upon the eve of the battle of Fredericksburg? Pickett's Division is said to be captured nearly entire. Oh, most wretched of calamities, worse than the loss of our capital, that the noble and invincible army of Lee should be hewn and hacked to pieces by a vile host of Yankee hirelings.

We determine to push on further South, in the hope of joining the shattered Southern army and participating in some more fighting.

I am listening to an escaped officer who asserts that he was with the army when Sheridan's cavalry rode in and dispersed their ranks. He says he saw whole regiments scattered and mingled in inextricable confusion along the roads, looking in vain for food and a commander. He describes how the Yankee cavalry rode them down without mercy, and how this and that general fled in dismay. Concluding that this talker is a gasbag, I leave him and go else where for information.[2]

Stragglers from Lee's army are flowing by us in crowds. The army is completely disorganized, and every one for himself is the sole idea. We borrow a mule from a negro boy named Hiram.

On this borrowed nag we move briskly and soon approach Pannill's Bridge, through a portion of the State that has never felt the scorching breath of war or drunk the warm life blood of the South's bravest men. Here rise tall fences enclosing rich pastures, fields of waving wheat

[2] Note that the events here described took place a few days before the surrender at Appomattox.

and sprouting corn. But the plenty scattered here appears in strange contrast with the desolation and exhaustion of the rest of the State.

No Yankees are as yet in sight but our own cavalry are straggling across the bridge by scores; also the infantry skulking from their regiments, invalids, trumpeters, etc. The country is full of deserters, and, judging from his detached forces, the army under Gen. Lee's immediate command must be reduced to a few thousand men. We heard cannonading all the morning in the direction of Appomattox station and the stragglers report that Lee lost 60 pieces of artillery and is retreating upon Lynchburg.

Hiram Loses His Mule

Arriving at Riceville wet and weary we fall in with a pressing gang who demand our fine and faithful mule for the service of the Confederate Government. We are at first disposed to resent this highway assault, but the pressing officers are polite and impressive, shewing us their papers and orders for doing this forcible deed. Upon examination we find their papers correct and part with our valuable friend with much regret. In order not to incommode us too much these agents of the government give us a small lazy and almost broken down affair (in the shape of a mule) and giving Hiram (the colored boy, donor of the mule) $10 extra we prevail upon him to take us five miles further on our route. Poor Hiram! the large tears trickle down his cheeks at the thought of his lost mule and he frequently bursts out with, 'What'll poor old massa say about this thing?' He beats the present mule unmercifully however, partly I suppose because the beast is slow, partly to smother his indignation and in sorrowful remembrance of the other which was so much superior to his present successor. . .

We stop for the night at the house of a Mr. Jackson.

While we are drying our clothes by a large log fire his daughters prepare a meal for us which is to be considered dinner and supper together.

Giggles for Supper

The three daughters, one grown, another about 15 and the third about eleven. While we are eating these young damsels come in the dining room, gaze at us for a while, titter and then retire; this amusement they keep up until a late hour of the night, coming to the door and peeping through the cracks, giggling, and running away.

We proceed towards Danville, accompanied by Mr. Jackson's young son. . .

By and by young Jackson points out a house by the road side where he thinks we can get some apple brandy. We enter and a nice and gentle woman with a sad expression of countenance consents to sell us a pint (for accommodation sake), but is far more concerned for her absent husband whom she fears has been killed in the recent battles. A little infant lies sweetly sleeping in its crib and smiling in its sleep, and an older child is making great sport with the cat upon the floor, both unconscious of their father's death and their mother's woe. We divide the brandy, but I think young Jackson gets the largest share for he very soon after as we resume our journey shows unmistakable signs of elevation; doffing his hat and twirling it high in air he puts his nag to redoubled speed and bids us follow him.

The Break-up of the South

As we approach Danville the roads become thronged with stragglers of all descriptions, wagon loads of people and their effects, moving into Danville, and crowds moving from the town. No one appears to have any settled conviction of what they are going to do or what the government is going to do. All is confusion and panic. Jackson in spite of his father's commands, urged on by curiosity and the desire of another treat, and the apple brandy god impelling, takes us all the way to Danville. Here not finding any places open where we could treat him, we send him back giving him 5 dollars with which to treat himself. I doubt a little if he got back safe with horses and buggy, for such articles are in constant demand by many loose and roguish stragglers.

Danville is in a perfect uproar. The President and his Cabinet were here last night and hearing officially of Lee's surrender left these parts for Greensboro, N. C. It is even reported that he has been captured, for a strong body of the enemy are said to be between this place and Greensboro.

CHAOS!

There is now no doubt of Gen. Lee's surrender which it is to be feared will be the closing act of our bloody tragedy. Poor Richmond! Poor Lee! Poor Army! Poor Confederacy!

The streets are choked with government wagons trying to force their way out of town. Soldiers and officers of every degree and description throng the town, mingled in one promiscuous mass, every one asking and but few answering. Some hurry by to take this road, saying it is safer; others seek an exit from the opposite side of the town. Here is an immense crowd at the depot and they are carrying off every thing transportable,—bales of cotton, wool, bundles of raw cotton, boxes of licorice, anything so it is substantial and capable of being moved. No chance to leave the town by the cars. The track has been torn up and Mr. Davis and party only escape capture by one hour.

What shall we do, cut off and hemmed in in the little town of Danville? The Commissary of the town is most liberally dispensing his stores to all who will take them, and the Quartermaster's stores are being equally distributed. Large crowds of savage and blood thirsty looking stragglers parade the streets and appear awaiting an opportunity to do some ugly deed.

What To Do? Then—A Decision

We get a very good dinner at a hotel which, wonderful to see and say, has not closed up; and after dinner Frank[3] and I are roving over the hills after horses wherewith to mount ourselves, Frank having learned from some of his quondam friends where to search for such animals. I am soon wearied with roaming about, but Frank is indefatigable in his exertions, the bare mention of a horse being sufficient to excite his nerves to the highest pitch.

I leave him and return to the hotel where I had left my valise. At the hotel I meet Mr. Adair Pleasants of Richmond who tells me that he is almost certain that my Father and brother are both in Richmond. And now comes the question, shall I or shall I not go farther than Danville? Is not the Confederacy fleeing too fast for one on foot (with a valise and no money) to keep up with it? Most assuredly it is at present, and I fear it cannot recover from this blow. Still, as long as I am an officer in the C. States army I feel in honour bound to follow the fortunes of the Confederacy until its cause is hopeless or its hopes of success revive.[4]

Lt. Rice swells our little band to four (also a prison comp.), and as we move on to the outskirts of the town Capt. White, 5th Va. Cavalry, also of prison memory, hails us to wait for him, and tearing himself away from a bevy

[3] Frank Jackson, son of the hospitable gentleman mentioned on p. 178.

[4] There is a hint here of another (and perhaps the chief) reason why Dooley undertook this trip southward: he felt his place was with the still faintly resisting remnants of the Confederate fighting forces.

of fair *admirers*, is soon trudging by our side, making our band five in number. A few hundred yards more and our party is again increased by no less a personage than a member of the Va. Legislature. Poor man, he has not a clean shirt in the world, nor script, nor bag, but thinks like poor 'Jo' it is necessary to 'keep a moving.'

A Heart-breaking Sight

Danville is only about a mile and a half from the N. Carolina border and 17 from Yanceyville, whither we intend going.

As we gain the open country a most mournful spectacle here and there greets the eye. In the gulleys and along the fences might be seen the abandoned muskets of the straggling soldiers. Some were broken, the barrels of others bent and the muzzles choked with mud. And cap boxes and cartridges lay in sad confusion along the road side. I had been in the retreat from Boonsboro and Sharpsburg, but never had my eyes witnessed so sad a sight as this. And my heart sinks low, for here lie unmistakable evidences of a set determination upon the part of hundreds to fight no more, and a shameless indifference as to whether the world knows it or not. By these signs more than by any others I seem to feel that the Republic is despaired of.

Dark clouds are gathering over the sky and large drops of rain beginning to fall. The thunder is rolling heavily over head and the lightning flashing vividly to warn us of an approaching storm. We are in constant dread of being captured and for this reason we are glad not to delay along the road.

Hospitality at Bowe's

After repeated short rests and invigorating draughts from Lt. Blair's large flask, as the crimson dawn stands blushing in the portals of the East, April 12, 1865,[5] we arrive near a large farm house possessing evident signs of the most ample abundance. Surely, said we, Bellona's car has not thundered down this road, nor the scorching breath of war seared the fresh harvests of their spacious fields. Just look at the chickens and turkeys and geese! The pork and the cattle and barns filled to *protrusion!* So we agree that if there isn't a chance of Breakfast in this house we had better give up traveling at other people's expense.

We are cordially received by the master (Mr. Bowe) of this house. A large decanter of the best apple brandy I ever tasted is set before us as an appetizer for our coming breakfast. And although we had been *sipping* of this fascinating beverage all the previous night, still, out of compliment to Mr. B. and his decanter we are obliged to taste it *anew.* An ample board was spread for breakfast and you may imagine we behaved very rationally and becomingly upon the present occasion.

After Breakfast we remained awhile having a social chat with Mr., Mrs., and Miss Bowe. Mrs. B. had seen something of life and had lived long enough to have grown old in her hatred of Yankees. She remarked that she thought herself a pretty good Christian, but if the Yankees *and white people* were going to be all together in heaven, she believed she'd rather not go to heaven at all. . .

We continue our journey towards Greensboro, partly on foot and partly with the aid of another borrowed mule and buggy.

Our mule is incorrigibly lazy, and when Blair and I mount the conveyance it is impossible to induce him to move faster than a very slow walk. The heaviest kind of a

[5] The very day of the Stacking of the Arms at Appomattox, the last day of the official existence of the Confederate Army.

switch was applied and worn to shreds but to no purpose. Exasperated beyond bounds, Blair affixed to a stick a common sized pin and inserted it gently into the beast's haunch, who instantly let fly his hind hoofs against the leather front of the buggy and started off at a tearing pace and gallop for some hundred yards, when he resumed his creeping pace.

The Pin Seems Finally to Have Been Forgotten

Repeated applications of the pin are necessary to enable us to keep a head of the walking members of the party. And our pin becoming bent, we drive up to a gate upon the roadside where there are four young ladies whose bright eyes and flowing ringlets might prove a temptation to any young man to cause him to stop and talk, *even though* he didn't want a pin, as we really *did.*

These young ladies are trying to (and dying to) hear the latest news from the army, and are frightfully shocked and alarmed to hear from us that there is no doubt of Gen. Lee's Surrender. No such idea had entered their heads. They were certain it would have turned out false, etc. The little one with ringlets tells us that they are sisters and refugees from Richmond and delight in the name of Barnes. 'Then,' said Blair, 'Do you recognize my companion, who is also from Richmond?',—*meaning me and not the mule.* One of them immediately exclaims, 'He must belong to the D—— family, for he favors them very much.' Upon which I apprise this highly gifted and intelligent young lady that she could not have surmised more accurately had she puzzled her head for a century.

We continue to converse at the gateway courteously, modestly and becomingly (for they all seemed to be very lady like, nor would they, I am sure, have remained at the gateway, speaking with strangers, but for the perturbed state of the Republic and their laudable but excessive anxiety to hear 'the latest' and render all the service their feeble voices were capable of to the gallant heroes of the Confederacy who are in such numbers fleeing from the State in order to choose another and a better position for the exhibition of their valour and the intimidation of their foes.

Mutual Encouragement

And our topic of conversation naturally enough being the late reverses of our noble State, Captain, and Army, we agreed with these young damsels that it was a down right shame for people, as many were doing, to talk of giving up our glorious struggle and submitting to the ignominious bonds of Yankee slavery. What though Lee had been defeated? Still every Southern heart must beat unsubdued and animated should each strong arm be to battle to the bitter end; and even if the war-scarred veterans should fail in their noble efforts, the very women of the South should rise up to expel the hated invaders from the Soil. With many assurances that such feelings would ever animate our hearts and that we should never despair of the Republic as long as a single straw floated upon the scarlet billows of this Sea of carnage, we bade adieu to our charming young acquaintances and hasten on our route.

Another Conversation on the Affairs of the Republic

We walk for a mile or so and are again forced [?] to stay our eager footsteps by the appearance of another cluster of fair maidens who are just as solicitous concerning the welfare of the Confederacy as were those with whom we had just parted. With these we exchanged many kind words and many assurances of future success and of the great exploits they might one day learn had been performed to immortalize our individual names forever encircled in the blaze of our country's glory. Then, our mule and buggy disappearing in the distance, we bid a reluctant farewell and stride away after our mule. When leaving them, Miss Totten, one of the fair damsels, presented me with a purple flower (of which I know not the name, perhaps a hyacinth) which I instantly transferred to my button hole, and it emits a pleasing fragrance all day.

Once more our journey is resumed, with a stop after a few hours at the home of a Mr. Brown. . .

As we enter the parlour a gentleman advanced in years and seated at a table lifts up his silvered head, saluting us kindly and enquiring what news from the turmoil of war and the clashing steel of contending armies. In his hands he holds a Latin author which by a closer glympse [sic] I discern to be Cicero,—Cicero's orations against Cataline. Happy and fortunate old man, thought I; how blessed is your lot, far from the din of battles and the war of civil commotions, here amid these rural shades you pass the declining years of a quiet and well spent life, surrounded by rustic simplicity and in the full enjoyment of a classic education.

Thanking Mr. Brown for his kind hospitality we hasten to overtake our companions. The brandy meanwhile begins to have its effects upon Blair, and he becomes very loquacious. He has gold coin sewed in different portions of his garments, nor is he satisfied until I put my hand upon his clothes and feel each individual piece. This information he would impart to only me, and, said he, 'this gold, this yellow coin is to be common property, should our party come to want, etc.!. . .'

We continue further southward through Caswell County,

North Carolina, and come to a crossroads general store, owned by Mr. Neal:

Mr. Neal is certainly a kind-hearted man and a thorough business man for all that. In the course of conversation I discover that he is a business customer of my father, and he shews me a case of goods received but a few days previous from my brother, probably among the last articles of merchandise that left Richmond before its Surrender. It seems strange to meet, away down here in Caswell Co., N. C., some one whom I had never heard of before and who has goods and a letter but a few days old from my folks in Richmond. While Mr. Neal goes to consult his wife and see if he can possibly spare his yoke of mules for our transportation, I write a few lines to the old Folks at home, bidding them farewell it might be for years and it might be for *never*.

The Case of the Seventeen Stranded Maidens

Resuming our journey we approach after some hours a nice looking house where we ask permission to stop and parch [boil?] our coffee. A youth of about 17 years of age comes to the door and invites us in. He says we shall have all the hospitality he can afford and at the same time informs us that he is in a wretched state of mind; for his tutor is absent from home and has left him in sole charge of the house, that he has some 17 young ladies on his hands, most of them strangers to him, and how he is going to provide places for them to sleep in that house he doesn't know. Poor youth! How I do pity that youth! 17 young ladies! Poor fellow! How they happened to fall to his lot he didn't tell me, but assured me that he felt the full weight of his responsibility, and I believed him.

Still Headed South

Our object is now to move South as quickly as possible, keeping ahead of the Confederacy, which is established for the present in this little Union hole of Greensboro. Here are Mr. Davis and his cabinet. General Beauregard and Johnston and Johnston's army are a short distance from the town. In the hospital at High Point we meet a Confederate soldier with his arm amputated. The poor fellow is very cheerful, laughing and talking, and says he feels the loss of his arm only when he thinks of his wife and child, dependent on their Yankee despoilers for their daily rations. Continuing towards Salisbury our journey is perilous because the country through which we are to pass is said to be infected with swarms of Bushwhackers, who are sworn enemies to the Confederacy, being nearly all deserters from the Army and living on plunder. . .

We put up for the night in the very strange home of Mrs. Coppels and her daughters.

It is a very poor looking house. Upon our request for lodgings, the old widow woman was very much put out and said it was a shame for people who had so much house room as Mrs. Sacristi[6] had to send stranger folk to her (Mrs. Coppels') poor lodging. We thought so, too, but it being now dark night and the rain beginning to fall again, we beg her to give us any accommodations she can, and we will be satisfied. So she said she would do what she could, and introduced us into a large room serving the purpose of kitchen, dining room and bedchamber and parlour.

An Unusual Feminine Accomplishment

Here before a large fire we dry our clothes, and afterwards are entertained by Mrs. Coppels' three daughters, sharp and stout country lasses, who *dip* snuff quite freely and openly, although they say they observe great modera-

[6] Mrs. Sacristi, just down the road from Mrs. Coppels', had refused the strangers admittance.

tion in this intoxicating pleasure *to what* some of their fair neighbors do.

As I never had seen any one dip I am not only amused but disgusted. And their manner of dipping is this: They have a large paper of powdered tobacco and three dogwood sticks (some inches in length and *chawed* into brushes at the end) in the paper. Every ten or fifteen minutes these damsels, who are all seated on a large bed, put this paper of snuff in their midst. Each one takes her dogwood brush and dipping it in the tobacco, inserts it into her mouth, touching first the tongue and then rubbing it around the teeth, gums, and roof of their mouth. After rubbing away until their appetite seems to be satisfied they drop the brushes back in the snuff, and place the parcel aside until next desired. The old woman we do not see take any of this enjoyment. Probably she has broken herself of the disgusting practice.

Rather Formidable Hostesses

The girls are nearly grown, good looking but very coarse in words and manners. They are sitting on the bed and appear by every look and gesture to hurl defiance at our party; and they keep close together as though united to repel any attack coming from our quarter. I am sure however that there is not a single one of us who is bold enough to attack these fiery and able bodied amazons. We adopt the conciliatory style and after one or two ill timed assaults had been repulsed with loss (for they have sharp and witty tongues, these girls), and by and by a mutual and implicit truce being agreed upon, they cease all hostile demonstrations and enter into amicable conversation, so that after a substantial but coarse supper they propose to dance a 'Scotch-a-round.' But our education being neglected in respect to this never-to-be-forgotten and graceful accomplishment, they good naturedly undertake in a few words to initiate us into the mysteries of this wonderful dance, and we are soon *au fait* in all its circumvolutions, and hop around in the most approved Highland mode.

The Tact of Mrs. Coppels

After dancing till we are thoroughly tired, the old widow invites us to retire. And while she is preparing our shake-down in an adjoining room she screams out, 'Yous soldiers generally have so many lice about yous that I hardly know how to fix for yous!' The vermin are the very things we are fearing ourselves, for we do not bear any of those tantalizing animals about us at present, and finding from the aspect of our shake down I think we may not be so free from the creatures in the morning.

Lullaby from the Weird Sisters

When closing our eyes for repose, the three sisters, our Dryad companions of the evening, join in chorus from the adjoining room (making night hideous), making the rafters of the old house ring with the melody of some ancient Methodistical chaunts. It would be vain to attempt to do justice to the voices of these wood Nymphs. Their strains are incomparable, and we sink into the arms of gentle slumber convinced that such melody we never heard before.

The Cat Who Broke the Ice

White is still rubbing his scratched hand from a little scrape he got into in the early part of the evening. It was while the girls were still holding an offensive attitude towards us, and White in order to smooth things over as much as possible began to smooth a pussy cat's back and got severely scratched for his pains. The girls enjoyed his mishap exceedingly as also did the rest of us. But White was dismayed and confused, and contributed much by his scrape to get us out of our scrape with the wood nymphs, who were more affable afterwards to us. . .

We are on the road again, and stop next at the house of Mrs. Daniels.

Mrs. D. gives us a most abundant supper. And I have noticed that in all the houses in N. Ca. where we have taken our meals, even the poorest families have an abundance of eatables. They may be coarse articles, but there is no lack of food, whereas in Virginia even in the wealthiest households many of the luxuries and ante-war abundance are missed from the table. Another thing we notice, that at breakfast and supper as well as at dinner we nearly always find pastry pies upon the table. . .

The next leg of our journey is to Salisbury, about 19 miles distant from Daniels'. . .

We passed a party of Bushwhackers, all armed with rifles and stationed at the fork of several roads. Six or seven in all they were quite a formidable body, and I am sure they were all deserters from our army. As they looked severely and suspiciously at our little party we thought we had best go over and speak to them. They were desperate looking fellows, all of them, and answered our questions a little doggedly. They were waiting there, they said for *horse thieves*, who had been stealing mules and horses from the neighborhood; and woe, said they, to any fellow we catch!

Among them is the most deformed man I ever saw. He has small portions of hands in arms of unequal length and size, the longer of which is about 1 foot and a half. His legs are mere stumps deformed in the most hideous manner, upon which he can in no wise stand. He says he can ride pretty well, and there is a horse present for his especial convenience. Why he is with this band of desperadoes I can't say, unless it be to identify stolen horses, etc. Feeling very much relieved that we have no horses with us whereby we may attract suspicion, we move on our road rejoicing.

Confusion in Salisbury

Approaching Salisbury we meet many country people bearing off the remnants of half ruined articles, such as pieces of machinery, half burnt cotton, wool, etc. Stoneman[7] appears to have destroyed immensely in the town, and the ruins are still smoking. And people in crowds are around the destroyed works, trying to save things from the smouldering wreck. The streets are very quiet and there are a few straggling soldiers to be seen here and there. Officers, too, there are, who appear not to know where to go or what to do. Several Cabinet members are at the Boydton House, where we will rest our weary bones for awhile. . .

We finally secure passage on a train bound for Charlotte.

The rail road is thronged with straggling soldiers, all dejected, all conquered, all going South, all anxious to get a place upon any passing train. It is past midday when we succeed in getting a foot hold upon a densely packed train. After proceeding a few miles the train runs off the track and we are obliged to get off and run for another several yards ahead. We succeed in scrambling to a place upon the tender, sitting upon the wood to be consumed. Every portion of this train is crowded to excess. Inside the travelers are packed both sitting and standing, and the platforms, roofs, and even the engine room are filled. So great is the throng that the Engineer is unable to work the engine and

[7] The reference is to the cavalry raiders of Federal Major General George Stoneman.

we are delayed until nearly dark before getting under way; and what a weigh we have!

A Cheer for Jefferson Davis

President Davis and his retinue have just passed us on horseback. As he passes a hearty cheer bursts from the mass of human beings thronging our train, and the president of his fallen country lifts his hat in polite acknowledgment of our respect and sympathy. Oh, but this is a sad sight withal.

Rail Travel Not Quite Normal

We proceed slowly towards Charlotte and every time that wood is needed we have to get off the tender and jump on again as soon as they have 'wooded up.' Such a journey I have never made, and we are frightened nearly beyond measure lest the whole crowd be precipitated down some cliff or thrown off some bridge. As we near our journey's end we are stopped, and upon inquiring the cause discover that we have made a narrow escape. The train a few hours ahead of us had been thrown from the track by the removal of a rail and 3 men were killed and 7 injured. Some think the rail was removed by Union enemies, who expected Mr. Davis and his Cabinet would be on this train. Others say that stragglers who had been refused a place on the cars had taken this diabolical means of revenge.

Desolation in Charlotte

We make the best of our way into the town of Charlotte, arriving here between one and two in the morning. No hotels are open and our footsteps echo through the silent streets as we pass along, and awaken in our own breasts hollow feelings of desolation and woe. Stoneman's raiders are said to be nearby and are expected in the town before day break. If so, the sleeping townsmen are not much concerned at his near approach, for they are sleeping so soundly that we are unable to gain admission into any home, not even Mr. Kerr's hotel.

We finally secure some hospitality from Mr. Kerr for old acquaintance's sake—Mr. Kerr's deceased son having been a friend of Col. Kernan, of our party—and we debate with ourselves, next morning, what to do next?

The government is completely disorganized, and can support neither its soldiers nor paroled officers. The only organized body of troops that have made their way from Virginia are Duke's and Vaughan's brigades of cavalry. Their officers are, many of them, jingling their spurs around the hotel and with abundance of silver in their pockets, living high, etc. How they have obtained this specie I don't know, but I suppose they have either captured it or it has been paid to them by the government, which probably had not means of transportation for all its specie and therefore distributed some of it for safe keeping with these troops who have for their brave and close adherence to the fortunes of our Fallen Republic the best right and title to receive *some* pay. . .

Being informed that 'Bob' and 'Lee,' old prison friends, live some miles out in the country, I desire very much to reach them, for I am perfectly wretched here in Charlotte, having no one and having no claim on any one for bed or board; but it appears to be impossible to get to my prison friends and I am more than ever thoroughly disgusted. I think the best thing for me to do is to go back to Richmond; but suppose I can do that, what then? Will not they be all beggars like myself? Oh, what a wretched condition of affairs we are all plunged in by this unfortunate war.

Decision to go Back to Richmond

I meet a young fellow from Charleston. He says he is going back to Richmond and insists that I go back with him. I think I'll do it. It is madness to go farther South, and going back does not present a very encouraging prospect. Imprisonment, starvation, all kinds of dangers, sufferings, and death in many forms stare me in the face.

The Refugees

The town is rapidly filling with straggling soldiers, officers, government officials, etc., many of whom declare their intention of pushing on to the trans-Mississippi. Since morning hundreds have crowded into the town from the direction of Salisbury, and every hour brings more. Houseless and homeless like myself, many of them, they know not where to go or what to do.

Startling News From Washington

President Davis arrives this afternoon and makes an address to a large number of people and soldiers. He has just received a telegram from Gen. Joseph Johnston to the effect that Abraham Lincoln the president of the Northern States was assassinated upon the 14th inst. (Good Friday) at a theater in Washington City, and that Sec. Seward was stabbed in his own house the same night and is not expected to live.

The most intense excitement prevails throughout the town upon receipt of this intelligence, and people don't know whether to rejoice or to be sad. And the reason appears to be that they are not sure whether it be better for the South that Abraham should be king, or some Successor. But whether they feel glad or other wise there seems to pervade the minds of nearly all a horror for the crime by which the monster was got rid of.

The people may be glad that a tyrant—a puppet if you please—the tool of a party whose life long aspirations and untiring efforts were directed with fiendish malice to the destruction and annihilation of millions of their fellow citizens, and whose designs have been carried out with a venom and malignity which their originator and instigator the arch fiend alone could prompt, the people may be glad that this tyrant has fallen.[8] But, that he died in his sins and by the assassin's weapon, leaving the taint of suspicion upon Southern men or upon this government, may be sources of regret and even of horror. Moreover, this novel and mysterious mode (novel in this country) of ridding society of obnoxious individuals cannot but awaken feelings of terror and intense distrust in the breasts of all well disposed citizens who may well fear lest the practice because of frequent occurrence and the stealthy blow of the assassin take the place of free speech and open accusation formerly granted to the people and to the press.

The Temptation to Despair

All I desire is to get home, and I am so worried all day about the means. Never before have I felt so much distress of mind and never have I felt so utterly abandoned. One of my great difficulties is being extremely sensitive and therefore unequal utterly to the present emergency. For, where others feel perfectly at home boarding at the expense of others, I am perfectly miserable lest I am unwelcome and a burden. Still, in the present crisis I must in consideration of my *stomach* assume a little more *cheek*. This morning I go to Mass and feel much better and more at ease for having done so.

Rumors

Many silly rumors are going the rounds today and posted upon the bulletin board in the middle of the town. Seward it is said cannot possibly survive, and is at the point of death if not already dead. Andrew Johnson, in terror of

[8] The structure of this sentence presents some difficulties.

the consequences and the vengeance of the infuriated North, has fled the country. The whole North is in confusion, anarchy. The Peace party are fighting the Republicans, Grant's army is disbanded, etc., etc.

'The Smash Up . . . Is Irretrivable . . .'

Gen. Echols in command here orders all paroled prisoners to leave this town for Augusta, Ga. What am I to do now? Never a go; I am not going to Augusta, Gen. Echols, and don't think you have any right to *say so.* And it is extremely hazardous to go towards Richmond, for the disbanded army are running wild all over the country, stealing, plundering, murdering and seizing trains of cars whereever they can find them. There is no order, no organization anywhere, and the government does not pretend to control the actions of any individual or collection of individuals. All is chaos and confusion and it is very evident that the smash up is irretrivable.

Upon returning to the hotel we observe a crowd gathering before the President's door (who, by the way, has quarters in a very shabby looking house) who, it is said, is in close consultation with Gen. Breckenridge just arrived. The crowd calls lustily for Gen. B., who comes to the door and with grace and dignity excuses himself from addressing them, and retires.

There appears to be no doubt of the existence of an armistice between Johnston and Sherman, and the death of Abraham the First. He ruled a saucy nation for 4 years, but assassination finally ruled him. The state of the country is frightful at present. Murder, rapine, and other foul crimes are rife in the land.

Gen. B. declares in a speech to Duke's Brigade that the adjustment of our difficulties will not be as favorable as might have been expected, but that they will be such that no one need be ashamed of them. They are trying to mollify our bitter discomfiture and crushing humiliation.

Gallant, But Too Late

Mr. Davis says nothing to *us*, nor appears abroad. He is opposed to peace measures, especially such as we will obtain from the North. His cabinet are all against him, seeing the futility of trying to resist when throughout the South scarce a respectable body guard of organized troops can be found to protect his own person. Mr. Davis believes that farther South the people will rise again and flock by thousands to his standard. Poor President, he is unwilling to see what all around him see. He cannot bring himself to believe that after four years of glorious struggle we are to be crushed into the dust of submission. Oh, it is a bitter, bitter draught and will torture our proud natures with the most excruciating agony, if it spares vitality itself.

The Sins of the South

And if the people blame Mr. Davis for their woes and humiliations, let them remember that his measures were taken for the best, he did all he could, and if he failed it was not only owing to his own errors and those of his cabinet. The chief cause of the failures rests with the people. Yes, with the people, for the Southern people have been false to their country. Had Mr. Davis received the support of the Southern people as Mr. Lincoln did that of the North, our armies would still hold a proud and defiant attitude in the field and our government stand upon a firm footing.

Talk, sirs, of the devotion of the women of the South! But we have seen enough of the women throughout the sections we have visited to convince us that the angry complaints and dissatisfaction of those at home caused numberless desertions from the army, and brought back desperadoes upon their State to harass the true Southern people and impede the machinery of the government.

Lukewarmness on the Home Front?

We have seen upon our route evidences of abundance which, had the people been true to their government, had furnished plenteous rations to the fagged and starved armies in the field. NO! Force has been employed *of late* to effect everything that the government wanted; and if the people have censure to cast on their President they should remember that he desired to do all in his power for them, and that in many cases they did all in their power to thwart him.

Plans for the Future

Go to church in the evening and recite the Rosary. Why should I seek any longer to follow the fleeting vanities of the world? Has not everything that I have set my heart upon turned out contrary to my desires and expectations? What has my religion always taught me but that worldly desires and pleasures bring with them only bitterness and remorse, and if I had followed the inspirations of my College days and entered the Society of Jesus, would I now be exposed to the misery, wretchedness and homeless wandering from which I now recoil and in vain endeavour to free myself? My anchor had been cast firmly and securely in a port that ever shall be calm and unagitated by the outside storms and cares of life. Where I may live in happy seclusion while Republics fall, empires totter to their ruin or civil wars boil and seethe around my hallowed precincts! If I ever find my way safely out of this turmoil and debris of our ruined fortunes, God has given me light to direct my footsteps whither I may repose in the enjoyment of His service and love and where with infinite patience and goodness He has been awaiting my erring and wandering soul through long years of sin and ingratitude.

The South is Prostrate

April 24th. The whole country seems to be steeped in a fatal lethargy, unwilling or unable to resist or forward anything. Every one is content to permit approaching events to take an unimpeded course no matter what results may follow. Groups stand around the street corners listening to the news and rumors, but no one asks what's to be done? All ask what has been done or what we may expect next? No Head, no body; the Confederacy is dissolved.

Though the Birds Sing—

This Charlotte is a sweet little town and Spring in all her loveliness is here, breathing freshness and fragrance through the rose bordered streets. Adorned with nature's purest ornaments, her spotless brow bedecked with garlands of the rarest hues and most refreshing purity. Smiles of love and joy play round her rosy lips. Green branches begemmed with emerald buds and bending boughs of luscious fruit extend their wavy arms to greet their mistress and their Queen; and countless Songsters from the grove and thick-set hedges burst their very throats to hail with gladsome notes their coming Love. Ah, sweet birds have you no pity in those straining breasts for the woes of a fallen people? Are ye all unconscious of the miseries and afflictions beneath your very eyes? Ye seem only to know that your beloved mistress has come and with her advance the advent of Peace is near. Peace! When no longer the shrill clarion shall pierce the quiet vale, nor cannon roar from hill top and mountain pass, nor the smoke of battle roll up from southern fields. Peace! ye celebrate in warbling ecstacies; be it honorable or dishonorable ye know not, can not; happy birds, would that we too knew no difference! No; though the birds sing merrily it is a sad day for our country, for the report is that terms of peace may only be obtained by 'A reconstruction of the Union.' Again lulled into false security by Yankee promises we may too soon regret our confiding faith, and but few years elapse ere a second war be waged for the self same principles that we have now failed to vindicate in years of the bloodiest war on record, and to end in naught but poverty, devastation, wholesale butchery and degradation.

Northward Again

Hearing that a train will leave tomorrow morning for Salisbury, I determine to try to make my way back home as best I can. All hope appears to be lost and we must submit to what ever terms the North may see fit to impose upon us. What terms will be is only a matter of conjecture. Nothing to be hoped from the Republicans!

April 25th [28th?], 5½ A.M. I eat a good breakfast, and bidding all my friends adieu and provided with a Snack prepared by my kind little hostess I mount an almost broken down freight train bound for Salisbury and begin my homeward route, and a dreary road lies before me but withal I feel more satisfied and my mind is more at ease, having a fixed purpose. I have several regrets in leaving Charlotte, first because I am leaving a really sweet place, where I have renewed and formed several pleasing acquaintances and have met with so much kindness; also because I am leaving here the last remnants of our glorious little Confederacy which, crushed to the dust, is utterly unable to resist the infamous tyranny and subjugation of her enemies; and am leaving behind all the fond hopes we had so long cherished of the future of our Republic, shattered and irretrivably lost, around which (unlike the Vase of which the Poet sings) no sweet odors linger; at least at present *they don't.*

Mr. Davis it is reported goes to Augusta today. He will make another effort there to rouse the inert, listless people, and may succeed in rousing some latent energies to action. Let us hope the best. . .

Our freight train proceeds 'at a most leisurely pace' northward. . .

At China Grove the straggling soldiery threaten to press our cars to take them back to Charlotte, but there is not enough of them to use force and they desist from their attempt. . .

We have a stop-over at Salisbury for the night, to wait for the next train which leaves in the morning. . .

I wander around town towards dark and perceive several doors of residences wide open, and gentlemen sitting upon the door steps whom if I only asked I am sure would give me a night's lodging; but I can't overcome myself so much as to say the word. Now if these gentlemen were living only a few miles in the country I wouldn't have the slightest hesitation in asking hospitality; but just because they live in a town I can't bring myself to the point. I suppose every one nearly of us has felt a freedom from restraint when dealing with, talking, meeting, etc. people in the country. The very fact of being outside the town appears to give you a right to address anyone you meet and you are always so kindly met in return that you never have the fear of the least rebuff. How this happens I shall not here try to account for, but shall merely say that I am this evening in the most forlorn and most wretched state of mind I have yet experienced.

This night I sleep on the floor of the office of the hotel. . .

April 26. After a restless night, and frequent disturbance by rats, as soon as the grayish dawn preceding the Saffron Morn with early blushes spread, begins to struggle thro' the dusty window panes of the office, I go forth and with some difficulty succeed in washing at the pump a little distance from the door of the hotel.

I take a long walk outside the town, watching the rising of the glowing orb of day and inhaling the fresh fragrance of early Spring. All is fresh and green and gay, for birds from every tree and bush and hedge are trilling sweet notes in praise of God and His works. Oh God! Who can stand and move 'mid nature's walks and not acknowledge Thy sovereignty and Thy Glory (of which the glory of nature is but the faintest shadow), and not praise Thee and bless Thee as the Author of all they enjoy and the End and Center of their Eternal aspirations.

I eat my breakfast in the fields—two biscuits, 12 days old, and two sugar cakes of the same antiquity are my allowance this morning. I tell you, this is no Joke.

I secure a place on the train for Greensboro.

Just before leaving the town a large lot of shells buried beneath the ruins of the depot begin exploding, some being thrown to a considerable distance; and we are literally shelled out of town.

Reach Greensboro 4 P.M. Everything in confusion. An attack has just been made upon the Quartermaster's stores by stragglers, which was repulsed by a guard of Johnston's army. Great excitement prevails and the Quartermaster is giving out shoes, etc. to those who ask for them. Stop-over at Greensboro tonight.

Ruins . . . of a Fallen Republic

April 27. I walk around the town this morning and the relics of the departed Confederacy remind me of the abandoned remains of some *large circus* which sometimes when a child I used to move among when the tents had been struck, the horses gone, their gaudy trappings no longer visible, and feelings akin to sadness would creep into my young heart, as I looked upon the remnants of what had been its glories, now all, all departed.

But now in the bitterness of an older and more disappointed heart I gaze on the ruins of a fallen Republic. Countless fragments of government papers, receipts, transportation papers, etc., etc. strew the ground in front, in hopeless confusion. Ah! proud land, what hast thou suffered, struggling in the throes of a mighty revolution, and for what hast thou endured thy agonies! If amid this universal desolation the cheering form of Liberty would emerge bright, glorious, and triumphant, oh! what a reward would she not prove to the haggard war-worn veteran; a recompense even adequate to these past long years of bloodshed, devastation, and ruin. But no! From this mournful wreck and frightful ruin the foul and unseemly head of despotism towers above its destined victims, and like some polluting monster with sharp rapacious claws clutches its shrinking prey and trails its accursed and venomous slime over all it grasps and sways and destroys.

Leave Greensboro 1 P.M. and travel *slowly* towards Richmond, but after effecting *10 miles in two hours* we reach a break in the road (a bridge broken down) and it is impossible for the cars to proceed farther. No cars to start from the other side of the break. Walk 5 miles to the next station. No trains here and after some delay I start for next station 9 miles distant.

I meet some old comrades on the march. We amuse ourselves by distinguishing the ownership of hound packs according to the tones of the hounds' baying.

We arrive at Foster's 10:40 P.M., having marched, baggage on our shoulders, 22 miles since 3 P.M. We put up at the home of my old friend, George Bethel. . .

I go down to his fields with George to watch the negro hands at work. There are a number of them ploughing, planting, and covering up corn in the same field. They are working with a will today, women and men altogether; for if they finish this patch of ground before 12 o'clock they are entitled to rest for the remaining portion of the day.

How the South Treated its Slaves

I asked George what they do the rest of the day, and he shewed me upon a portion of the farm their own little patches, which the Negroes take a pride in cultivating and have a right to all produce by their own ground. Every Saturday afternoon, as today, each one devotes some hours to the care of his own garden. Happy creatures whose bliss is greatly owing to their ignorance; but the restless spirit of New England has spread its wings on the blast, and its envenomed breath has gone forth to poison the happiness of black and white.

It is Cold This Spring

April 30. Sunday. Cool and beautiful morning. The fowls from the barn yard and the birds from the thickets unite in chorus to celebrate peace . . . peace to a blood-stained desolate land. But, alas, a peace of submission, a peace whose sweetest breathing is empoisoned and rank with tyranny. Oh! this is a cruel, cutting stroke into the very heart of Southern pride. Bow down, now, crushed Southern hearts; bow down the head to receive the servile yoke which the money making puritan [sic] has so long yearned to place upon thy neck. They have the power now; how long they shall be permitted to use it the good God only knows, who has allowed them to take it and will wrest it from them in good time. Oh, joyous Spring, so lovely, so fresh, so fragrant, and fair, thy sweetest smiles cannot cheer the heart of the conquered man.

May 1, 1865. Lovely May is peeping through the crimson of the East, radiant with smiles and suffused with blushes; fresh from the late April showers she comes tripping o'er the lawn spreading odours on the balmy air and sprinkling roses as she moves.

Observation on Southern Families

George Bethel is extremely lazy, but neither his brother Wm. or his Father is of indolent habits. I believe in most Southern families that are well to do there is nearly always one son constituting the sporting member of the family, who makes it his especial business and duty to keep up the honor of the house by fine horses, hounds, talking of his ancestry, etc., and to do nothing else; and people who write so much about Southern pride, wealth, and indolence, take their impressions generally from these worthless but petted members of the family.

Observation on Federal Guards

May 2. Maj. Bethel goes to Danville this morning to procure a couple of men as a guard for his house against the encroachments of the straggling blue coats, who venture nearer and nearer every day. He will bring me back word as to when I can return to Richmond. He returns late in the evening bringing with him two blue coats to guard the premises. They are coarse, brutal, unmannerly fellows, Yankees, and expect to be treated as a portion of the family. Mr. B. has already misgivings about the prudence of his conduct, and is like the man who purchased the elephant; *but he has two*, and both spit tobacco juice over the floor and request to be supplied with liquor, whose *temperate* use they despise.

Finally we start towards Danville.

On the way we stopped at a lady's house, whose beautiful little girl brings us a glass of water, and whose fierce snarling mastiff could scarcely be restrained from throttling us. I remarked to Willie[9] my companion that the house seemed very desolate and the lady and her daughter to live by themselves. He said yes, that the lady was a very kind and gentle person, but had a Northern husband whom the neighbors would scarcely have anything to do with on account of his coarseness and brutality.

A Brief Tribute to New England

Along the road we pass many negroes deserting their masters and going to Danville to search for those blessings so liberally promised them by Uncle Abraham and the whining hypocrites of N. England.

Schedule Subject to Change Without Notice

May 4. I proceed to the depot,[10] determined to wait all day in order that I might not miss a train if one should start spasmodically; for this is frequently the way they do now: make as many persons as they can deceive believe that they will not move for some time, and then when people are off their guard, off they go!

I finally get a place on a train. It goes about half a mile towards Richmond, then returns to the station. Next morning we are still in Danville.

May 6, 5 A.M. We enter a train of cars that it is thought may possibly go to Richmond. After an hour's delay we find that the probability of our getting to Richmond de-

[9] Identity not clear.

[10] At Danville.

pends in great measure upon the disposition of some one to run the train. Only one conductor can be found, and he cannot think of going because he declares he *would be in Richmond on Sunday without a clean shirt*. But he is gradually coaxed and finally some gentlemen promise him that they will see that he gets a dozen clean shirts if necessary to wear on Sunday. . .

8½ A.M. We are moving briskly towards Richmond, and about 12 in the day I step off the train and proceed up the street.

I shall not attempt to describe my feelings. The city in ruins and the hated and triumphant army of our malignant foes marching through the ruined city. With a raging headache and a swelling heart I reach my home, and here the curtain falls. . .[11]

[11] This entry of May 6, 1865, is the last one of the diary.

EPILOGUE

BUT, for John Dooley, the curtain had not fallen. As he had mentioned two or three times in his journal, he had long wished to study for the priesthood. Only a few months after his coming home to a desolate and mourning Richmond he entered the Novitiate of the Jesuit Order at Georgetown, September 1865. In his new life he found spiritual peace. Afterwards, when assigned to teach the small boys in the preparatory division of the college, he "knew how to mingle firmness and kindness in such a way as to win the respect as well as the affection of those under his charge."[1]

His war experiences, however, had taken a far greater toll of his strength than he suspected. From the very first days of his life in the Novitiate he was afflicted with a serious indisposition of the lungs; from the latter portion of 1868 onward he was forced frequently to spend weeks in the infirmary. He died at Georgetown on May 8, 1873, nine months before the date set for his ordination to the priesthood.

The few extant records of this latter portion of his life reveal the same traits as manifested in his war journal. He is a very human person, with warm feelings. Also, amid considerable sufferings which befell himself and his family, he was unostentatiously very brave.

The war had seriously affected the elder John Dooley's business. By early 1868 the family appears to have been in

[1] *Georgetown College Journal*, Supplement, June 1873, p. 72, quoting the *Catholic Mirror*, Baltimore, Md., n.d.

considerable financial distress. The son reveals his feelings in a letter from Georgetown, Feb. 9, 1868:

. . . And now, dear Father, I must offer you . . . my deepest sympathy in all your troubles—and so many—and let me tell you again that it was one of my greatest impediments when about to leave for the Novitiate that I was to desert you in the very midst, as it were, of the storm, to desert you when you would seem to have most need of any little service I might have been able to give. But in a generous letter, the exponent of a generous and sacrificing will precious in the sight of God, you gave me up freely, bidding me do that which God bade me engage in; and signifying that if his Will was accomplished you and Mother were happy in its execution. You made the sacrifice and our Lord has blessed it. I know he has, and if you do not feel it now at least you will feel sure of it in the future. During the past gloomy period, gloomy at least for the conquered, your business must have suffered much, and, indeed, according to the accounts of affairs in Richmond I can scarcely understand how you have been able to carry on any business at all. However, what can we do but hope for the best and work for the best and pray for the best? I wish I had some consolation to offer, something which would cheer you up. But what can I offer you? In my little troubles, whenever I have any, the only relief I find is in complaining to our Lord in the Most Blessed Sacrament. He is there always patient, always kind and ready to assist and console us. In His adorable Heart tho' deprived of every exterior comfort we may always find riches without limit and interior consolation which shall infinitely surpass the pleasures of earth. Pray for me, dear Parent, and if I cannot console you more, be assured that I wish to do all that I can. And now most earnestly begging your prayers night and morning, I remain your loving son, J. Dooley, S. J.

Two weeks after writing the above, John experienced a double sorrow of distinctive keeness. His father had suddenly died; but John himself, being confined to the infirmary, was unable to go to Richmond for the funeral. We may imagine his feelings as he wrote this letter to his mother; under the circumstances, it was the most he could do to comfort her:

Georgetown, Feb. 24, 1868

My dearest Mother: What can I say to you, what can I write to console you in the depths of affliction? I can think of nothing, since there is nothing but your ever unshaken faith which can sustain you in such a trial. Oh, Mother, it came suddenly, sadly enough upon me. What a shock must you and the family have experienced. All day yesterday I sat in my room, oftentimes going over in my mind how this one or that one bore up against the sorrow overshadowing the house. All my grief has been for each one of you. Our Lord has consoled me in many ways, perhaps especially so since I was unable to make the journey . . . Oh, Mother, you may not weep if he enjoys more happiness than we, if the bursting the bonds which bound him to material things now permits him to roam in a region of happiness where sorrow is unknown, where pain is never felt, where joy, peace, and the love of God alone reigns. And does it not seem that the one who is left upon earth is the one most abandoned, most to be pitied? Before beginning this short note I intended to beg of you not to give way to grief, not to give way to the sorrow which would so naturally oppress you in this your deepest affliction. Oh, Mother, I have been thinking of the rest; what would they do without you? . . . Then I implore you (although I seem to be doing an impertinent and superfluous thing) to struggle on against troubles and grief and affliction of every kind for their sakes who always looked to you for counsel and consolation in their doubts and trials. Dear Mother, I will now close these few lines, awaiting still further particulars. I am still confined to the Infirmary but am much better than some days ago. I remain as ever with the most heartfelt Love and sympathy for you and all the family. Your loving son, John E. Dooley.

A letter to his brother James a few days later gives a

hint of another touch of pathos in their father's death at this particular time:[2]

. . . I am glad Florrie's Marriage came off in time, for although it was a Sad thing to leave the Marriage Altar to attend the death-bed, yet it appears to me it was much better thus, than waiting six months longer. Give my love to each one of the family and tell them that I desire to express to each my most heartfelt sympathy and that I feel far more than I can express . . . How do Sadie and Josie bear up? No doubt like brave hearted girls. . .

It is not only the note of grief, however, which marks John's letters from Georgetown. The essentially gay and hopeful spirit which had carried him through so many toils and perils of war, had not deserted him. He has matured, his profession has turned his thoughts in a spiritual direction, but he is the same 'Jackie' Dooley, with the same lively and cheerful interest in little human things. He tells his mother in a letter of May 5, 1868, that,

. . . being freed from Infirmarians' medicines, etc. I am again occupied in the performance of my usual duties. I am now prefect among the junior students . . . My health continues good and I trust will sustain me a long time yet, provided it is the will of our Lord. I am among the small boys, and twelve years ago I was a small boy myself here in the same Dormitory, same Study Room and Class Rooms. How things have altered since then . . . Pray for me incessantly nor let the others forget me in their daily prayers, especially during this bright and glorious Month consecrated to the B. Virgin whilst numberless altars are adorned with the sweetest flowers and hearts are encircled with bright gems of devotion and the incense of prayers ascends almost uninterruptedly to the throne of our Queen. Oh may yours and the childrens' hearts expand with love and confidence towards Her, and find in Her sweet smile of approbation the joy of heaven on

[2] John to his brother James, from Georgetown, March 5, 1868.

earth, and in the unfathomable depths of Her loving, compassionate Heart true consolation in all your pain. Recommend me to Florrie [just married] and present her with my warmest congratulations upon her happiness. Remember me also kindly to Willie [her husband], and give my fondest love to each member of the household. . .

In a letter to Florence, November 9, 1868:

. . . I was delighted to hear of Willie's good crops, and wish with all my heart that they might be fifty times as abundant; and I unite with you all in thanking God for His kind Providence over you in this as in many other respects. You must let me know how each thing succeeds and keep me posted in all that regards the farm . . . Remember me kindly to all of our Valley[3] friends and tell Willie he must write me a long letter (when at leisure) full of details and how he (calkerlates) to get along under the present administration . . . Tell Mrs. Lewis [Mother of Florence's husband] not to forget the promise Jim [John's brother] made her of the *finest bonnet* in Richmond. . .

As the years went on, John's loved ones were not strangers to sufferings. Financial losses due to the war necessitated many family readjustments, and brought many an hour of anxiety. Meanwhile John did his best to strengthen those at home by means of his letters. He is careful not to add to the family worries by mentioning much about his own state of health; but gradually there emerges from his correspondence the undoubted fact that his lung ailment is growing steadily worse. One receives the impression that as time goes on he is better able to comfort those who suffer because he is experiencing suffering himself. Nor does he ever lose his note of cheerful courage and hopefulness. He writes thus at the beginning of 1872:[4]

[3] Florence was living at Sweet Springs, Va., in the Shenandoah Valley.

[4] January 2, 1872, from Georgetown.

My dear Mother and Josie:
I wish you both a most happy New Year and many returns . . . Judging from Mary's letter last month, they appear to be in no little trouble at the 'Sweet' [Sweet Springs]. But what can we do? Patience is all we have to defend ourselves against such afflictions. Prayer must do an immense deal of good but we must wait patiently for our prayers to have their effect . . . All your letters give me great consolation and enable me the better to bear my own little crosses with more resignation and courage. Let us thank our Divine Lord that while He has sent us afflictions and pain He has also given us the Grace to feel that they are the gifts of His mercy and not the scourges of His anger. Oh, who would live and suffer patiently did he not know and feel the mercifulness of each stroke and expect the rewards of eternity for his pain? Since no one approaches the inmost sanctuary of the Heart of our Loving God until sanctified and purified by suffering, we may well receive crosses and afflictions with sincere joy, for it brings us nearer and more similar [i.e. makes us more similar] to that Divine Sufferer Who began his existence amid poverty, neglect, and pain, and Who ended a life of deepest sorrow and anguish in the agonies of Crucifixion. You must not think of me with emotions of sorrow for I am doing splendidly in health and our good Lord will perhaps give me strength enough to be ordained. Once ordained I shall be all right, for all our weak and despaired of scholastics recuperate after their ordination. . .

Withal he has not lost his tender interest in the more happy aspects of life at home:

. . . Tell Josie she must tell me how tall she is; what books she is studying; what are the *leading fashions* for girls of fourteen, how many girls of her own age she knows in Richmond; the names of all the Boarders at Arlington [where Josephine was attending school]; the proprietor's name, etc., what routine (daily) is in vogue in the house; *what fare is there* and, if there be room, how the boarders are dressed at meals? Also the singing at St. Pete's

[St. Peter's, Richmond, the Dooley's parish], if she sings in the Choir, etc. etc. . .

In a later letter[5] he returns lovingly to the subject of Josie, who, with her mother, had recently paid a visit to Georgetown:

. . . I was very much pleased with Josie, not so much with her looks as with her goodness of heart. She is not at all pious, but so that she be really good, loving towards her own, and faithful to our Lord, I don't think we can reasonably ask for more. She offered me one of her pictures and she was the only one to whom I had not given one of mine; so I gave Ma one of mine for her in parting. . .

From the latter part of 1872 onward, John's physical condition became steadily worse. His last extant letter was written to his sister Mary on Christmas Eve of that year:

. . . I wish you all a happy Xmas and would that I could make it truly happy for all in every respect. I had fondly hoped that Ma would ere this have been able to write to me, but I must bide my time and hers also, I suppose.[6] The weather is very cold and I have been afraid to venture out during the past three days. Everything has a bleak wintry appearance; about three fifths of the boys have gone home. In consequence of which we will not have solemn high mass tomorrow; and upon the whole the exterior Christmas promises to be a cold one here. The interior Christmas however will be as genial as the fervour of our hearts admits. So that Jesus the Infant Saviour has a warm welcome for all in His poor grotto at Bethlehem . . . Pray for me often and let me know what can be done about the family pictures; and if I can scrape up from north, east, and west one of each, no matter how old it may be, the older the younger! Love and a happy Xmas to Ma and Jem and Sister Sallie. As ever, your loving brother, John.

[5] John to his sister Florence, July 16, 1872.
[6] Mrs. Dooley had been ill.

On May 8, 1873, he died in the infirmary at Georgetown. A few days before the end his mother, his sister Josephine, and his brother James were summoned to his bedside. During his last week of life, apparently, he could speak only with great difficulty; so, in expressing his thoughts and making known his needs an old habit was reverted to—he made jottings on a slip of paper kept on his bed-table. On this small page—really the last of John Dooley's diary—there are but half a dozen entries. It is indicative of his character that the first of these is a bit of news about a baseball game at Georgetown, while the last is a manifestation of concern for the convenience of his brother:

May 1st. Ugly day and rain prevents the Stonewall and Quickstep match.[7]

May 2. Another bad day with rain.

May 3. Another bad day. Brother Jem pays me a visit.

Please get some water.

Vitriol at twenty minutes less than 1 P.M.

Did my brother go out? has he reading matter? will he remain over night?

"Cheerful to the last conscious moment," said the *Georgetown College Journal*, "he expired peacefully, and without a struggle. In his last sleep, his face wore its sweetest smile. He was followed to his grave in the College Cemetery by a concourse of the faculty and students. His mother, brother, and sister were also present at the obsequies."[8]

[7] These were two teams made up of the students at Georgetown.

[8] *Georgetown College Journal*, supplement, June 1873, p. 72.

APPENDIX I

Lines Written in Memory of Willie Mitchel, Youngest Son (17 Yrs.) of John Mitchel the Irish Exile. Willie Was Killed at Gettysburg While Carrying the Colors in Pickett's Charge.

Bright in his genius and bright in his youth
    Gone to his grave!
No Sisters to tend him, no mother to soothe,
    No arm to save.

Gone from the comrades and friends he loved best,
    Gone to his doom!
Gathered from earth and forever at rest,
    Gone in his bloom!

Fell mid the crash and roar of the strife,
    Gasping for breath!
Fell where the bravest had sacrificed life,
    Grappling with death!

Died with his banner encircling his head,
    The staff by his side!
Mid the smoke of the guns and thickly strewn dead
    His death moan was sighed!

Dead midst confusion defeat and dismay,
    Piled with the slain!
No hero more noble this terrible day
    Presses the plain!

Still in death's arms with wide gaping wound
Calmly he slumbered!
No more in our strife at the bugle's shrill sound
Shall he be numbered!

The brave stranger rests neath the red clotted field
With thousands around!
But the tears that loved ones from broken hearts yield
Fall not on his mound!

When the storm rushes on the mountain oaks moan
Sad o'er his head!
But still to the loved ones that spot is unknown
His cold narrow bed!

No tall marble shaft adorning his grave
Speaks of his fame;
But his warrior friends when they speak of the brave
Think on his name.

Fresh be the verdure that springs round his bed
Fragrant and sweet!
May the angels of heaven pillow his head
At Jesus' feet.

* * *

APPENDIX II

"Prison Reminiscences (of the war between the states), Johnson's Island, Lake Erie, near Sandusky, Ohio."

A few verses written while in prison upon several of the writer's messmates. We were twelve in a room during the last 6 mos. of our imprisonment—6 bunks, 2 in each of three corners of our room, and two lodgers in each bunk. [There follow the names of the twelve, with their places of origin.]

These were my messmates, and amusing myself upon certain nights I got off some verses on each [messmate], which, although almost perfectly nonsensical, I wish to preserve in humorous remembrance of those who for so long and so patiently endured together with me the hardships, tediums, [tediousness?], and cruelties of prison life on Johnson's Island. . . . .

I begin ex abrupto therefore with a few verses on Lt. John Steptoe (an estimable young man) who was one of the best chess players, controversialists, and upholders of religious tenets that we had in the prison. Lt. Steptoe and Capt. Jones bunked together and not unfrequently [sic] at night would have a family quarrel concerning the positions that either might assume whilst asleep and which resulted in inconvenience to one or the other.

Lt. John Steptoe

Long had he battled for the right
And stemmed the tide of Yankee might;
But vanquished by the fate of war
At length he graced a captive's car,
And here by Eries' lonely shore
Lists pensive to the billows roar,
Or plays at chess a matchless game
And keeps alive his deathless fame;

For 'tis conceded without doubt
That Steptoe and his Pawns can rout
(And we have many skillful men)
The best of players in the Pen!
'Tis Sad, but yet 'tis true, alas!
O'er which I'd fain in silence pass,
That Jones and he cannot agree
How each should fix the bended knee
When each beneath his blanket lies
And Slumber presses on their eyes.
('Step always planted his knee in Jones' back.)

Jones loq. at midnight:

'Now Imps of darkness press around!
And yet I hear no boisterous sound!
'Tis but the fancy of a dream
With which my heated brain doth teem.
But still I feel them pressing *here*
The flanking[1] imps are in my rear!
What ho! ye devils clear the track!
O pshaw! 'tis only Steptoe at my back!

Why *do* you push and shove so hard,
For my backbone hast no regard?
Do, Step, be done! Remove your knees
From off my back, Sir, if you please!

Step. loq.:

What sounds are these at dead of night
That Slumber put to rapid flight?
What, Bawler! what afflicts you so
That thus obstreperous you grow?

[1] During our war all its science was reduced to a process of Flanking.

'Tis not enough to groan and snore
But would you make disturbance more?
For Shame! unhappy man restrain
Your tongue, nor bawl so loud again!

Jones:

I tell you, Step, you've got your knees
Screwed in my back—and that must cease!

Step.:

Must cease forsooth, and you must take
A space as wide as all the lake;
If you but keep your chosen side
The bunk for two is plenty wide!

Thus speak these heroes in the dark;
But at the singing of the lark
They both awake, forgetting all
Last night their drowsy tongues let fall.

Lt. William Henry Keiningham

We called him 'Pete'. In prison he was my messmate and bunkmate. He was sincere, trustworthy and honest to scrupulousness in every affair he ever undertook.

Where Seven Hills Majestic rise
And lift fair Richmond to the Skies,
Where booming cannon hoarse resound
And Mars in fury stamps the ground,
There did our gallant hero Pete
First stand upon his tiny feet.
As years revolving quickly flew
In size and strength our hero grew,
Till war's fierce raging flames arose

And he went forth to meet his foes.
Three years did battles round him rage,
As fierce as e'er the bloody page
Of history shews from Moses' age
Down to the enlightened wars *we* wage.
Twice wounded on the battle plain
At length he swells the captives' train;
And here where Erie's billows rave
And day and night this island lave,
Our Keiningham is safely stored
And lives and sleeps on hardest board.

. . . .

In Chess good Wm. doth excel,
At least he plays extremely well.

. . . .

But I am sorry that you've shaved
Those hairs which 'neath your nostrils waved;[1]
I trust they soon will wave again
And to their former growth attain;
And this I fear me much they'll do
Before Exchange will send us thro'
To glad the heart of many a friend
And strength to all our armies lend.

Captain Jefferson Waggener

A small man, afflicted by the loss of one eye. The life of the room—full of wit and good natured, although inclined to be gloomy when the 'exchange' question was discussed. He was perhaps 40 years of age with a tendency towards baldness. All his acquaintances called him 'Wagg' for short, because he was a wag.

[After informing us that Waggener comes from Kentucky, "A land of teeming fields and fertile vales, . . . Where bouncing

[1] Pete had a very long red moustache.

farmers ride around To feast their eyes upon their ground . . .", the poet continues as follows:]

Among the first who heard afar
The thunders of the coming war
Was 'Wagg', the Hero of my Song,
Whose name I've slighted now too long.
From Clarksville came this famous man,
Came with the 14th Tennessee,
An officer of some degree.
Encamped upon Virginia's soil
He underwent fatigue and toil,
And many months his trusty blade
Great havoc among the Yankees made;
He many hardships patient bore
Unused to which he was before.
To prison he came a year ago
With hesitating steps and slow.
Cards have become his greatest forte,
At which according to report
He plays a very skillful hand
And satisfies each just demand.
Good anecdotes he oft relates,
On lofty themes expatiates,
Gives all around a lucky hit
And sets us laughing by his wit.

[There are a few more verse-biographies in this vein.]

APPENDIX III

Sketch of the History of the 'Old First' Virginia Infantry Regiment[1]

The lineage of the Old First Virginia Infantry Regiment runs back to the Charles City and the Henrico Militia Regiments, whose first recorded muster occurred at Westover on July 12, 1661. This muster was a preliminary to the general assemblies, scheduled to take place at the various company stations in July and August, for the defence of the colony against the French and Indians. Major William Harris directed this mobilization and recruitment.

It is to be noted that the Charles City and Henrico Militia were drawn exclusively from the Richmond district, the same area from which was to come, at a later period, the First Infantry Regiment. In 1661, of course, the latter designation was not used.

Almost a century later, an important step was taken in the gradual evolution of the Old First. Governor Robert Dinwiddie, desirous of driving the French from the crucial position of Fort Le Boeuf at the head of the Ohio, determined to transform the militia of the Dominion into a regular regiment of volunteers. The various county lieutenants were to secure volunteers for this regular regiment. Major George Washington (later appointed Lieutenant-

[1] The present sketch of the history of the 'Old First' is based entirely on the researches of J. C. Weckert and H. G. Dickerson, *op. cit.* For the regiment's activities in the War Between the States, use has been made also of Charles T. Loehr's volume, already cited.

Colonel, with the Honorable Joshua Fry as Colonel)[2] was to command a company composed of fifty men from Lord Fairfax' Frederick Militia, and fifty men from the Augusta Militia of James Patton. The First Virginia Infantry Regiment was officially created on February 16, 1754, when the Virginia Council ratified this action of the Governor.

The Baptism of Fire of the First Virginia Infantry

The newly-formed regiment, comprising 306 men, left Alexandria in April 1754. They arrived at Wills' Creek in the latter part of the month, to be greeted by unfavorable news. The Ohio Company's party under Captain Trent had been driven from their half-finished post at the headwaters of the Ohio by Captain Contrecoeur with a sizable French force, which had immediately raised Fort Duquesne on the site.

Colonel Fry, gravely ill, handed over the command of the regiment to George Washington. The latter's plans were, at first, very cautious. He intended merely to establish a fortified position at the junction of Redstone Creek and the Monongahela (now Brownsville, Pa.). But learning that the French were advancing from Fort Duquesne with the apparent aim of attacking him, he determined to forestall his adversaries by attacking first. Pushing on to the Great Meadows, he encamped there.

On the morning of May 27, Washington was informed that the French were within five miles of his position. That night he made a forced march through a dense woods in a

[2] Fry was a native of England and a graduate of Oxford. He resided at this time in Essex County, Virginia. At one time professor of mathematics at William and Mary College, he later served in the House of Burgesses. With Peter Jefferson (Thomas Jefferson's father) he surveyed large tracts in Virginia. As a by-product of this work he drew a valuable map of the colony.

heavy rainstorm, to launch, the next morning, a surprise attack against the enemy in a depression on the upper fringe of the Great Meadows. The battle was won before dusk. "This," say Weckert and Dickerson,[3] "was the first blood shed in the struggle that was to end in the expulsion of the French and the supremacy of the Anglo-Saxon race in North America."[4]

Although it had clearly won the engagement, the American force was now outnumbered and in a precarious position. With a view to holding out until he could be reinforced, Washington fortified his camp at the Great Meadows, renamed Fort Necessity. Some reserve companies of the regiment did indeed succeed in reaching him; but when the French and Indians under de Villiers attacked in great strength on July 3, the Americans were obliged to fall back and surrender. De Villiers conceded honorable terms.

On its return home the regiment, far from being censured, received a vote of thanks from the House of Burgesses. The following year, the House began to pay pensions to the men disabled in the campaign.

Governor Dinwiddie, changing his military policy, now reconstituted the regiment on a basis of extreme decentralization. Henceforth the captains were to exercise a large degree of autonomous and practically supreme authority. Washington, declining to accept this change, resigned his commission.

[3] *Op. cit.*, p. 14.

[4] The same authors call attention to the fact that May 28 has been in several instances a momentous date in American military history. On May 28, 1758, General Amherst's expedition arrived at Halifax. The first contingent of the American Expeditionary Force sailed from New York on May 28, 1917. Exactly one year later our First Division began at Cantigny the first American offensive of World War I (*Ibid.*)

The First Virginia Regiment in the French and Indian War

At the time of Major General Edward Braddock's arrival at Alexandria on February 20, 1755, as Commander-in-Chief of the British Forces in America, the First Virginia Regiment had been enlarged to 1000 men.[5] An Act of the Virginia Assembly, August 5, 1755, provided for the retention and recruiting of the regiment, the entire force not to exceed 1200 men. This very effective force was, with others, engaged from 1756 to 1758 in frontier warfare against the Indians, Major Andrew Lewis being in active command of operations in the field, while George Washington was Commander-in-Chief of all the Virginia troops. During this period, it will be remembered, occurred the disastrous expedition of Braddock. Washington, on November 25, 1758, with a force of Virginians and Pennsylvanians, took Fort Duquesne, henceforth named Fort Pitt. At this period the Virginia Regiment had been raised to a complement of 2000 men divided into the First and Second Regiments. Washington retained command of the First; William Byrd was made colonel of the Second.

On his return to Virginia in December 1758, Washington resigned his command. That same month, the Second Regiment was mustered out. In January 1759 Governor Fauquier appointed Colonel Byrd to the command of the First, which was then sent to Southwest Virginia for service against the Cherokees. Colonel Byrd resigned in 1760, to be succeeded by Colonel Adam Stephan, under whose leadership the regiment was mustered out at Fort Lewis, Augusta County, in 1762. After being so discharged, the

[5] At this time the captains of the Regiment were: Thomas Wagener, —— Cock, Peter Hog [Hogg?], Robert Stobo, Adam Stephan, William Polson [Poulson?], William Peyronne, George Merver, —— Stuart.

men of the First and Second Regiments were still subject to call as a militia cadre of the colony's potential armed forces.

The First Virginia Regiment in the Revolution

On March 23, 1775, Patrick Henry arose in the Virginia Convention to demand "that this colony be immediately put into a state of defence." In carrying out this urgent plea, there was little delay. The Colonial Convention meeting in Richmond on July 24 of the same year, passed a law for reorganizing and expanding the militia. Patrick Henry was appointed colonel of the First Regiment and Commander-in-Chief of all other troops to be raised in Virginia.

The mustering point was Williamsburg, on a plain behind William and Mary College. The Henrico Company, Captain John Fleming commanding, was the first to arrive at the assembly ground, on October 14, 1775. This Company, it will be remembered, was at this time regarded as a unit of the First Virginia Regiment; the same was true of the Company designated the 'Chesterfield.' Both units were recruited exclusively from the Richmond area.

Friction between Henry and the Committee of Safety forced the resignation of the former from his two military charges. By August of 1776, however, all the Virginia regiments had been assimilated into the Continental Line, under the immediate jurisdict' 'n of the Continental Congress. As already described i the Introduction to this volume, the First Virginia Regiment took an active part in several of the major campaigns of the war.[6]

[6] The following were the commissioned officers in the First Virginia Regiment as of July 1775:

Colonel Patrick Henry.
Lt. Col. William Christian.
Major Francis Epes.

After the winning of independence came the necessity of reorganizing again the militia of the states, for purposes of a more strict uniformity. At the beginning of 1791 the militia representing the Richmond district comprised three sub-divisions—the Henrico, the Richmond City Militia, and the Chesterfield. In the following year each of these sub-divisions was given an autonomous status in what was now a more uniform state militia. The Henrico became the 33rd Regiment; the Richmond City Militia was named the 19th; the Chesterfield became the 23rd. The *name* 'First Virginia Regiment' was dropped, but the living constituents of the regiment were very much in existence.

This organizational plan of the Virginia regiments continued through the period of the War of 1812 and afterwards until 1846, when, in order to meet the special necessities of the Mexican War, the old First Virginia Regiment was recreated, with companies enlisted from all parts of the state. The Nineteenth Infantry (the old Richmond City Militia) furnished two companies to this revived Old First—the Richmond Grays (Captain Robert G. Scott) and the Richmond Rangers (Captain Edward C. Carrington).

Aide to Col. Henry: A. S. Dandridge.
Chaplain: Rev. M. Bland.
Surgeon: Dr. —— Hall.
Quartermaster: James Gault.
Paymaster: George Brooke.

Captains	*Companies*
Robert Bullard	Mecklenburg.
—— Campbell	not known.
William Davis	Princess Anne.
John Fleming	Henrico.
John Markham	Amelia.
William Sears	Gloucester.
Edmond Dickinson	Williamsburg District.
Thomas Nelson, Jr.	" "
Francis Smith	Chesterfield (1777).

The regiment served as train-guards under General Zachary Taylor in the Monterey campaign, but participated in no battles. It was mustered out on the declaration of peace in 1848.

Meanwhile, a spontaneous evolution was taking place in state troops throughout the Union. Instead of following their old custom of relapsing into inactivity or of being mustered out in time of peace, the state military organizations were holding meetings, drilling at stated periods, and keeping themselves alive as formally constituted volunteer citizen forces. They began to be called the "organized" militia, and were given various names in the various states. They were the "Volunteers" in Virginia, the "Line" in Maryland, the "Volunteer Militia" in Massachusetts, the "National Guard" in New York, and the "State Guard" in North Carolina.

This establishment of an "organized" militia in Virginia constituted a new and more thorough resuscitation of the Old First. By a General Order of May 1, 1851, it was directed "that the volunteer corps of the 19th and 179th Regiments and attached thereto, with those (if any) of the 23rd Regiment, Chesterfield, and 33rd Regiment of Henrico, shall from this date constitute a new regiment to be denominated the First Regiment Virginia Volunteers, headquarters at the city of Richmond. . ."[7]

The First Virginia in the War Between the States

The outbreak of the War Between the States found this reorganized First Virginia Regiment prepared for action. Colonel P. T. Moore had been elected its colonel in 1860. In April 1861 three of its companies were detached for

[7] Adjutant General's Office, Richmond, Va., May 1, 1851, General Order No. 1.

service with other units. The Grays, the first company to leave Richmond, were assigned to the 12th Virginia Regiment, which was then stationed at Norfolk. The Blues and Company F went to Frederick to drill recruits. These two Companies, after participating in several minor engagements, were used as nuclei for two other regiments, the 46th, and the 21st. The latter became later a part of General Stonewall Jackson's famous "Foot Cavalry." The remainder of the Old First, plus a company from Washington under Capt. C. K. Sherman, went into camp on April 27 at the new Fair Grounds, then known as the "Camp of Instruction."[8]

On May 24 or May 25 the 1st Regiment marched out of Richmond en route for the First Battle of Bull Run. At that time its commanding officers were as follows:

Colonel: P. T. Moore;
Acting Adjutant: Samuel P. Mitchell;
Captain John Dooley [father of the author of this journal], 1st Co., C, the Montgomery Guards;
Captain B. J. K. Lee, 2nd Co., B;
Captain W. O. Taylor, 3rd Co., I;
Captain J. G. Griswold, 4th Co., D;
Captain F. J. Boggs, 5th Co., H;
Captain Wm. H. Gordon, 6th Co., G;
Captain John Miller, 7th Co., K, the Virginia Rifles.

[8] A problem in discipline was created by the proximity of this camp to Richmond. Loehr, *op. cit.*, relates the following incident: "Sundays usually found the camp deserted. On one occasion there was only one man in Company D left to 'fall in.' When the drum beat for dinner the Captain, who was in his tent, called out, 'Fall in, Co. D'; to which the one man replied, 'Captain, must we form in one, or two ranks?'; to which the reply came, 'Of course, in two ranks.' When the Captain came out of his tent he found Private Craig standing alone, with his legs far apart, as he said, 'in two ranks'." (7–8)

A Glorious Record

On the famous July 18, 1861, at Bull Run, the 1st Virginia covered itself with glory. Years later, General Longstreet paid the regiment this tribute:

> The old First Regiment was with me at Bull Run on the 18th of July, and made the first fight of Bull Run, which drove the Federals and forced them around Sudley Springs. . . . The heavy part of the fight was made by the old First Reg't., so that it can well claim to have done more towards the success of the First Manassas than any one regiment. This, too, was their first battle, and I can say that its officers and men did their duties well, if not better, than any troops whose service came under my observation.[9]

After taking some part, though not a leading one, in the 1st Battle of Manassas (July 21, 1861), the 1st Virginia saw no more active fighting until the following spring. During the first few months of 1862 the actual command of the regiment was in the hands of Major John Dooley. During this period the complement of the famous unit was, from various causes, greatly reduced. The terms of service of many of the members had expired; there were some desertions; a considerable number had been drafted into "essential industries" behind the lines. It was therefore determined that a thorough reorganization and a new recruitment should be effected on April 21–26. As a result of this, the revised list of commissioned officers now read:

Colonel: Lewis B. Williams;
Lt. Col.: Frederick G. Skinner;
Major: William H. Palmer;
Captain, Co. B, T. Herbert Davis;
Captain, Co. C, James Mitchell;
Captain, Co. D, George F. Norton;

[9] Letter of July 20, 1883, in reply to invitation to attend annual reunion of 1st Virginia Regiment; quoted in Loehr, *op. cit.*, 11.

Captain, Co. G, Frank H. Langley;
Captain, Co. H, William E. Tysinger;
Captain, Co. I, J. W. Tabb.[10]

The regiment's next battle was at Williamsburg, on May 5, 1862. Here Private James Dooley, son of Major Dooley, was wounded and captured, then almost immediately paroled. At Seven Pines, May 31, the unit suffered heavy casualties. In the Seven Days Battle around Richmond, and in the engagement at Frayser's Farm (June 30–31, 1862) the Old First gallantly maintained its reputation.

The activities of the regiment from the early summer of 1862 until Gettysburg have been described by John Dooley in the preceding pages. After the fatal 3rd of July, 1863, the 1st Virginia was only the ghost of its former self; but it retreated with Lee's forces into Virginia, to take part until the end of the war, in the last-ditch delaying actions which were only postponing the final disaster. Near Petersburg, on May 16, 1864, the 1st and 7th Virginia Regiments were the first to break the Federals' right wing. On May 21 a part of the 1st held at bay the advance guard of Grant's armies. This enabled Lee to gain Hanover Junction first with his army, and foiled Grant's aim of forcing his way to Richmond by that route. On April 6, 1865, the Old First fought its last battle, at Sayler's Creek. It was stationed there as a forlorn hope, a rearguard action to save Lee's army. When the regiment surrendered at Appomattox on April 9 there were only 17 men in its ranks.

Later History of the First Virginia

Between the end of the War Between the States and the outbreak of World War I, the history of the First Virginia

[10] Major John Dooley was retired on account of his failing health. He was long past military age.

is not marked by any event of great importance. The first real reorganization of the regiment after 1865 occurred in 1871. In the Spanish-American War the First Virginia was again broken up, to be reorganized again in 1899–1900. It performed some useful services in the Richmond streetcar strike of 1903, when it was employed frequently to guard the hoses of the firemen who sought to extinguish the blazes set by the strikers.

Beginning, however, in the latter half of 1916, the Old First entered upon a new and important phase of its history. After a special course of training at Brownsville, Texas, under General James Parker, U.S.A., it returned home at the beginning of 1917 to revert again to its National Guard status. On July 25 of that year it was called to the Federal service.

World War I

Company B, Captain William A. Stack commanding, left for Camp McClellan, Anniston, Alabama, on August 17, 1917. Together with Company F, Second Regiment, of Roanoke, and Field Hospital, of Radford, Company B formed the vanguard of the celebrated Twenty-Ninth Division. In the final organization of this Division, the three Virginia infantry regiments formed the 116th Infantry. The First Regiment became the First Battalion.[11]

The First Battalion of the 116th Infantry took part in the great Meuse-Argonne offensive. In this engagement it was led into action by Major George M. Alexander. This officer being wounded on October 10, command of the

[11] The Twenty-Ninth Division was led by Major General Charles G. Morton, U.S.A., and was composed of the National Guards of New Jersey, Maryland, Delaware, Virginia, and the District of Columbia.

Battalion devolved on Captain Stack, the next in rank, who continued in this charge until relieved.

There is Much in a Name

On September 21, 1920, the 1st Battalion of the 116th Infantry became once more the 1st Infantry, Virginia National Guard, Colonel John F. Bright (later a mayor of Richmond) commanding.

But the regiment's vicissitudes in nomenclature were not yet ended. By an order dated March 9, 1922, the time-honored title '1st Virginia,' so redolent of a glorious tradition, was changed to the 183rd Infantry. The alteration was cordially disliked by the members of the regiment, as well as by the people of the state as a whole, who took so much pride in the historic recollections attached to the title 'Old First.' Colonel Bright was evidently a good diplomat, for, as the following document shows, he secured for his regiment and for his state, in 1929, the object of their desire:

War Department, A.G.O., 20th Feb. 1929; G.O.I., A.G.O., Va., 22nd Feb. 1929:

To perpetuate the history of the First Virginia Regiment, covering the Colonial period of our National Independence, and to permit its decendants more fully to enjoy the glorious traditions, as well as to stimulate emulation of the fine example of our first Colonial Military Organization, the request of the Regimental Commander, Colonel John F. Bright, that the numerical designation of the 183rd Infantry, Virginia National Guard, be changed to 1st Infantry, Virginia National Guard, was approved by order of the Secretary of War, by 7th endorsement, War Department, A.G.O., Feb. 20th, 1929 (AG 325.455 Va.) The designation of the 183rd Inf., Va. Nat'l. Guard, is accordingly changed to 1st

Inf., Va. Nat'l. Guard, effective this date, the birthday of George Washington, one of its former commanders.[12]

It would be pleasant to relate that this finally settled the matter; but such, unfortunately, was not the case. On January 1, 1941 the Old First, though without change of personnel, was renamed the 176th Infantry. On June 29, 1944, it was inactivated completely, and its members distributed among other units. After 'V' Day, it is hoped, the historic title will be reassumed.

[12] Quoted in Weckert and Dickerson, *op. cit.*, 46.

INDEX OF PROPER NAMES AND PLACES

INDEX OF PROPER NAMES AND PLACES

This index contains the more important of the proper names and places mentioned in the volume. Unless otherwise indicated or generally familiar, all place or county names are for Virginia.